TRAINING TO BE A
TOP GUN
FOR
GOD

DAVID REED

Table of Contents

Chapter 1

My Mission

Hello, my name is Shadow! I have been assigned the mission to encourage you to be a Top Gun for God. Only strong spiritual leaders remain on the straight and narrow pathway to heaven. Is that you? It can be!!! Because you can do all things through Christ, to include defeating Satan's evil tactics.

During my 22 years in the United States Air Force, I had the honor of serving as an Aggressor Air Weapons Controller, a role that would become one of the most defining chapters of my career. My tactical call sign, "Shadow," was more than just a name; it represented my mission and my commitment to excellence. In the Pacific Air Theater, where I was stationed, my squadron was unique—an elite group that was handpicked from the best of the best. We were the only flying unit allowed to wear our call signs on our uniforms, a badge of honor that signified our expertise and camaraderie.

Each member of our squadron was recommended for this duty by someone in another Aggressor Squadron, a testament to our skills and dedication. We were not just controllers; we were instructors, mentors, and warriors. Our primary mission was to teach U.S. and Allied flying units how to defeat the enemy, simulating real-world combat scenarios that demanded both strategic thinking and tactical proficiency.

The training was rigorous and intense. We pushed ourselves and our pilots to their limits, honing our skills in aerial combat and tactics. Every exercise was a lesson in adaptability, teamwork, and resilience. As we engaged in mock dogfights and strategic maneuvers, I learned the importance of anticipating the enemy's moves—an essential skill that would later serve me beyond my training.

The experience I gained in those skies became a model for how I would approach the challenges in my life, particularly in my spiritual journey. Just as I had to prepare pilots to face the complexities of aerial warfare, I realized I needed to equip myself to confront the more insidious battles in life—those that are fought in the shadows of doubt, fear, and temptation.

In the same way that I studied enemy tactics to prepare our forces, I began to study my own vulnerabilities. I learned that the greatest battles often occur within us, where the enemy is not a foreign fighter pilot but our own insecurities and fears. I applied the lessons of strategy and preparation to my spiritual life, understanding that to defeat Satan, I had to be vigilant and proactive.

I embraced the discipline of prayer and meditation, much like the pre-flight briefings we conducted before every mission. I sought guidance from scripture, drawing parallels between the battles in the Bible and the conflicts I faced in my daily life. Just as I had to trust my training and instincts in the cockpit, I learned to trust my faith as my guiding compass.

Through this journey, I found that the principles of leadership, teamwork, and resilience that I honed in the military were equally applicable to my spiritual battles. I surrounded myself with a community of faith, much like the squadron that had my back in the skies. Together, we supported one another, sharing our struggles and victories, and holding each other accountable in our spiritual walk.

Reflecting on my time as "Shadow," I recognize that my experiences in the Pacific Air Theater were not just about flying and combat. They were about preparation for life's greater challenges. The lessons learned in the cockpit became the foundation for my spiritual warfare, reminding me that while the enemy may lurk in the shadows, with faith, preparation, and a strong support system, we can emerge victorious.

Interestingly, this was six years before the release of the iconic Top Gun movie in the spring of 1986. My tenure as part of an elite squadron from 1980 to 1984 placed me in a unique position—one that few could claim. I was part of a Top Gun Squadron before it was popularized by Hollywood. While the glitz and glamour of the film would later capture the imagination of many, for us, it was a serious mission driven by purpose and dedication.

Being involved in such a significant operation, training U.S. forces and Allied nations in the Pacific theater to counter enemy air-to-air tactics, instilled a profound sense of pride. We were at the forefront of military innovation and strategy, shaping the future of aerial combat. It was exhilarating to know that our efforts directly contributed to the safety and effectiveness of our forces in the field.

Yet, amidst that pride, it was often a challenge to remain humble. The camaraderie and respect we shared within our squadron were palpable; we were a family, bound by our shared experiences and the weight of our responsibilities. However, the recognition we received could easily inflate egos. It was crucial to remember that our success was not solely our own but a collective effort—a testament to the teamwork and dedication of every individual involved.

When I got to be off my scope and in the cockpit, I learned that humility is not a sign of weakness but rather a reflection of strength. The best pilots are those who recognize their limitations, who are open to learning, and who understand that every flight is an opportunity for growth. This lesson transcended the skies; it became a guiding principle in all aspects of my life.

As I transitioned from the military to the next chapter of my journey, I carried with me the memories of those intense training sessions and the friendships forged in the heat of battle. The spirit of collaboration and the commitment to excellence that defined my time as "Shadow" became the bedrock of my future endeavors. I learned that true leadership is about lifting others up, fostering an environment where everyone can thrive, and recognizing that our victories are built on the sacrifices and contributions of many.

In the end, while the world may have come to know the thrill of Top Gun, for those of us who lived it, it was never about the fame or the glory. It was about the mission, the training, and the people who stood beside us, ready to face whatever challenges lay ahead.

As I continue to navigate the complexities of life, I carry those lessons with me, knowing that with faith, humility, and a strong support system, we can face any adversary—whether in the skies or in the shadows of our personal battles.

In the Aggressor life, there were sacrifices with glory that equated to a lot of time on the road away from our families.

I know most of you don't know what a Weapons Controller is, so I will try to educate you on my role. First, let me make clear that I was blessed to be on flying status for cross-training purposes. That meant if a back seat was available, and I had an up-to-date flight physical, and I was not on scope, I could fly. So, I was not the pilot; I was the guy in the back seat enjoying the ride. My part of the daily mission was to be the guy who watched the skies from a radar scope and would keep my team members safe from enemy threats.

Most of my flights were in the back seat of the Blue Forces F-15s or assimilated bomber mission T-33s, and I also flew with the Navy Top Guns at Subic Bay in their A-4s. Later in my career at Shaw AFB, I had the chance to fly in the backseat of an F-16 and achieved the honor of getting my 9-G pin (the tightest hug of my life).

I will try to explain my duties and their connection to the Air Force Top Gun School and how it led to my calling to be a Top Gun for God. As I talk about my military experiences, please do not think I am describing modern-day warfare. But if you are from one of our enemy nations, then everything I am about to say is exactly how we fight today!

Chapter 2

The Original Top Guns

(Photo Unknown Source)

Here is a group of the Original Top Guns from the old Wild West. Look closely, and you might see some names you recognize.

- Wyatt Erp

- Teddy Rosevelt

- Doc Holiday

- Morgan Erp

- Butch Cassidy

- Sundance Kid

- Bat Masterson

- Judge Roy Bean

I would love to have the opportunity to sit down with all those Top Guns from the Wild Wild West—those legendary figures who faced their adversaries with grit, courage, and a sense of justice. Imagine hearing their insights on overcoming the enemies they encountered in a time when the stakes were high, and the law was often just a whisper in the wind. Each gunfighter had a story, a lesson learned from the dusty trails and the confrontations that defined their lives.

Even better, I dream of saddling up with them, riding down those dusty trails, sharing tales of bravery and resilience, and discussing the future Top Guns—those who will continue the legacy of standing firm against injustice and evil. Together, we would explore the lessons learned from their battles, not just in the context of the Wild West but in the broader fight against the darker forces that seek to undermine our lives.

Let me clarify, however: I am not encouraging anyone to become a military combatant or to take up arms in the physical sense. The enemy I want us to confront together is not a man with a six-shooter but rather Satan, the embodiment of temptation, deceit, and despair that seeks to lead us astray.

As I reflect on the parallels between the challenges faced by those iconic figures and our own spiritual journeys, my hope is to inspire you to prepare for spiritual warfare. Just as the gunslingers had to be quick on the draw and sharp in their judgment, we, too, must be vigilant and equipped to face the trials that life presents.

In the Wild West, the stakes were high, and the outcome of a confrontation could hinge on a moment's decision. Similarly, in our spiritual battles, we must be prepared to act decisively against the temptations and trials that threaten our faith. We can learn from the courage of those who stood up for what was right, drawing strength from their stories to empower ourselves and others.

I seek to empower you with the tools to teach others how to achieve victory against the evil spirit of Satan. Just as the archangel Michael stood firm in the face of darkness, we too can earn the title of Top Gun for God, wearing it with pride as we engage in the fight for righteousness. Our battles may not be fought in saloons or on dusty streets, but they are no less significant.

As we gather together—whether in fellowship, conversation, or prayer—we can share strategies, encourage one another, and build a strong support system. We can remind each other that we are not alone in this fight. With faith as our foundation and the courage of those Wild West legends in our hearts, we can rise to the challenge, ready to face whatever adversary comes our way.

In the end, my desire is to inspire a new generation of warriors—those who will stand firm against the forces of evil, just as the Top Guns of the Wild West did in their time. Let us prepare ourselves for the battles ahead, armed with the knowledge and strength to confront the enemy that seeks to undermine our faith. Together, we can emerge victorious, not just as individuals, but as a united front against the darkness that threatens to engulf us. God describes His Top Gun, Michael, in the verse below.

Revelation 12:7: "Then war broke out in heaven. Michael and his angels fought against the dragon, and the dragon and his angels fought back."

Revelation 12:8: "But he was not strong enough, and they lost their place in heaven."

Revelation 12:9: "The great dragon was hurled down—that ancient serpent called the devil, or Satan, who leads the whole world astray. He was hurled to the earth, and his angels with him."

My mission is to make you aware of this enemy and the risk he is to our eternal destiny. As Top Guns, we have the power through God to say, "Fights On", "Kill", as we go offensive to Satan's evil plans.

Once I committed my life to Christ in December 1970, I put on the full armor of God and started my journey as a disciple of Christ to do my part to help fulfill the Great Commission. At that point, the Navy Top Gun program was just getting started, and no movies had been made yet to make Top Guns "cool". But God had plans to steer my life down unknown and unimaginable paths to bring this message to His family.

My spiritual journey has encompassed 55 years of devoted commitment to Christ, during which I have always used my home as a place of love and hospitality. Through countless home Bible studies, I have inspired others around the world to embrace the truths found in God's Holy Word.

Our roots started in a small apartment in Kentucky, to our on-base housing at Little Rock AFB, to dynamic experiences in Okinawa, Japan, leading youth in San Antonio, Texas and Florida, being a spiritual leader in a small church in the Philippines, Serving as an Elder of a small church in South Carolina, then 34 years of serving God's family in several Florida churches.

There was a time when I had 22 people in my home Bible study. Out of special needs, I created the One Love Family Bible Church for my home Bible Study Group. I did so because my group consisted of unchurched people and attendees from five different churches, all in one big living room. For the unchurched, I gave them a church family to connect with.

My home has always been a sanctuary of hospitality, a place where God's love was shared freely and where friends and family found encouragement in their walks with Him. It was here that laughter echoed through the hallways, prayers were whispered in quiet corners, and the warmth of fellowship enveloped everyone who crossed the threshold.

Each gathering, every meal shared, and each Bible study held within those walls was a testament to the love and grace that flowed from God through my heart.

In July 2024, after 34 wonderful years, I made the heartfelt decision to surrender my lakefront home in Eustis, Florida, and move to The Villages. This transition marked the end of a significant chapter in my life, one filled with cherished memories and profound connections. As I prepared to leave, I reflected on the countless moments that had shaped my journey within those walls.

To capture the essence of those years, I penned a poem titled "This Old House." In it, I poured out the memories, the laughter, the tears, and the love that had defined my time there. I included photos alongside the verses, inviting my readers to feel the spirit of the poem and to visualize the moments that made that house a home. Each image serves as a snapshot of the life lived within those walls—a visual reminder of the community built, the faith shared, and the love that flourished.

"This Old House" is not just a tribute to my physical dwelling; it is a parallel to the Christian homes we all aspire to create. It speaks to the importance of cultivating an environment where faith can thrive, where hearts can be nourished, and where God's love can be experienced in tangible ways. Just as my home was a refuge for many, I hope that each reader can reflect on their own experiences and the homes they have built or wish to build.

As I move into this new phase of life in The Villages, I carry with me the lessons learned and the memories created in that beloved home. I look forward to creating new memories and continuing the legacy of hospitality and love in my new surroundings. I hope to inspire others to open their homes, to share their lives, and to foster a spirit of community that reflects the heart of Christ.

In the end, "This Old House" is a celebration of not just a physical structure but of the relationships, the faith, and the love that make a house a true home. May it resonate with you and encourage you to embrace the beauty of your own Christian home, wherever that may be.

"This Old House"

This old house was just a place that we found to live one day,

It was built of concrete blocks, nothing special in any way.

It sat upon on a small lake with a small dock at the time,

It even had a swimming pool for the days the sun would shine.

A house does not give you any love or respect,

It cannot mend a soul or help a life that feels all wrecked.

But when occupied with God's family, the house seems to come to life,

It appears to have a glow and a heart that makes things right.

The reputation of this house seemed to build each passing year,

It was known for hospitality and bringing families lots of joy and cheer.

With friendly hospitality and love for all that came through its doors,

It became a special place for feeling loved and no one kept any scores.

The Mom and the dad were always sharing God's precious love,

It soon was apparent to all that it was coming down from above.

The mom who was the hostess served God's love to all that came,

And all her guests loved her, that is how this old house built its fame.

The mom was a teacher and was known throughout the town,

She had loved many children and lifted many frowns.

She was a great encourager, one who would always go the extra mile,

Just to make someone's day better and try to make them smile.

This special home would change with seasons as its hostess loved them all,

She had lots of decorations, some big and some quite small.

They all seemed to say this is a happy place to be,

Because God gives us seasons to enjoy new scenery.

She kept an accurate calendar of all her friends' special days.

That included birthdays and anniversaries that seemed to pass by like a blaze.

Her warm and tender heart made her guest excited to come in,

Whether Sports, birthday parties or Bible studies, no one wanted them to end.

This old house taught many people God's precious Word throughout the years,

It baptized young and old and helped dry up many tears.

Someday, this family will leave this old house, and the stories will be told,

How they loved so many people, and for Jesus, they stood bold.

Many children and puppies have run and played in its backyard,

For all those special memories will make leaving it very hard.

Mike Alstott, Tampa Bay Buccaneers, "A Train" playing quarterback for my grandson, Zane's, 10th birthday party

18

This old house is just a building that can be used for many things,

We just hope it continues to serve God's children and help them get their wings.

God, thank you for your blessings you give us each and every day,

Thank you for this old house we got to use along our way.

We can never fully grasp where God is leading us, but with every step we take and in every direction we go, it is all for God's purpose and His divine plan. Even during my time assigned to a Top Gun Squadron, I never imagined that those experiences would one day inspire me to write a book about being a Top Gun for God. The roots of this idea didn't blossom into a meaningful concept until several years after I retired from the Air Force.

It was during my time teaching a men's Wednesday night Bible class that the vision began to take shape. I had the privilege of leading a wonderful group of men who had been with me for a couple of years. Together, we explored the Scriptures, supported one another, and grew in our faith.

One evening in the spring of 2008, as I was teaching, something remarkable happened. The Spirit spoke to me in a profound way, and I found myself declaring that we needed to be Top Guns for God. I was momentarily taken aback by my own words, thinking, "Wow, what did I just say?" It felt as though the declaration had come from a deeper place within me, a place where God was stirring something significant.

However, this was more than just a passing thought; I realized that God had planted a seed in my spirit for me to nurture. While I wasn't entirely sure how to develop this idea, I understood that it was a calling rooted in my past experiences. Looking back on my life, I could now clearly see how the various places I had been and the training I had received were all part of God's preparation for this moment.

Crossing paths with such great men throughout my life has been a humbling experience. In the Philippines, I had the privilege of encountering many remarkable individuals, including the historical significance of places where General Douglas MacArthur once walked. My home on Clark Air Base was once an Administration Building he frequented, and I stood on the island of Corregidor, where he was famously rescued to avoid the Japanese invasion. These experiences were not just historical footnotes; they were reminders of the legacy of leadership, courage, and faith that I was called to embody.

As I began to embrace this new mission of being a Top Gun for God, I recognized that it was about more than just a catchy phrase. It was about inspiring others to rise up in their faith, to be leaders in their communities, and to confront the spiritual battles that we all face. Just as pilots are trained to navigate challenges in the air, we, too, must be equipped to navigate the trials of life with faith, courage, and resilience.

In the months and years that followed, I committed myself to nurturing that seed God had planted. I began to develop the idea of what it truly meant to be a Top Gun for God, drawing on my military experiences while intertwining them with the teachings of Christ. It became a journey of discovery—one that would lead me to write and share my insights, encouraging others to embrace their own callings and to live boldly for their faith.

In retrospect, I see how God orchestrated every step of my journey, preparing me for this moment of revelation. Each experience, each encounter, and each lesson learned was a building block leading to this calling. And it is with a grateful heart that I continue to seek His guidance, ready to inspire others to become Top Guns for God in their own lives.

In my journey of faith and service, I even purchased a home in Eustis, Florida, a place that would become a cherished sanctuary for my family and me for 34 years. Little did I know this home held a remarkable piece of history. In the early 1960s, General Douglas MacArthur himself had sat in the Florida room of this very house, enjoying the elevated views of the serene lake while smoking his pipe.

The thought of sharing space with such a legendary figure adds a profound layer of meaning to my time there. As I reflected on my life and the experiences that shaped me, I couldn't help but feel a connection to the legacy of leadership and courage that MacArthur represented. His presence in that room, contemplating the beauty of the landscape, seemed to echo the importance of vision and purpose—qualities that I strive to embody in my own life.

This connection to MacArthur served as a reminder of the significant paths I had walked and the lessons learned along the way. Just as he navigated the complexities of military strategy and leadership, I, too, was called to navigate the challenges of faith and service. The elevated views from that Florida room became a metaphor for the perspective we gain when we look beyond our immediate circumstances and seek to understand the greater purpose God has for us.

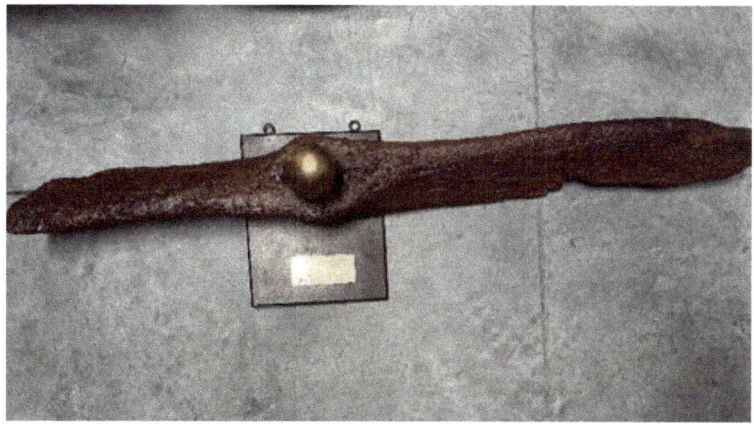

Interestingly, my journey took an unexpected turn when I found a remarkable piece of history while scuba diving around the island of Corregidor in Manila Bay. This island, steeped in the legacy of World War II, was the site where General Douglas MacArthur famously made his stand during the Japanese invasion. As I explored the underwater landscape, I stumbled upon a prop that was supposedly from a mail plane that had been shot down during that tumultuous time.

The moment I unearthed that prop, I felt an overwhelming sense of connection to the past. Here I was, diving into the very waters where history had unfolded, where decisions were made that would shape the course of nations. The propeller, now a relic of a bygone era, served as a tangible reminder of the bravery and resilience displayed by those who fought for freedom. It was as if the spirit of those who had come before me lingered in the depths, urging me to reflect on the sacrifices made for the sake of liberty and justice.

As I held that prop in my hands, I couldn't help but think of General MacArthur's legacy, the leadership he exemplified and the courage he displayed in the face of adversity. His determination to return to the Philippines after being forced to leave was a testament to his commitment to his country and its people. In that moment, I realized that my own journey, while different in nature, was also about returning—returning to my faith, to my purpose, and to the calling that God had placed on my heart.

This discovery further deepened my understanding of the interconnectedness of history, faith, and personal purpose. Just as MacArthur's actions were part of a larger narrative, so too was my life woven into the fabric of God's plan. The prop became a symbol for me— a reminder that our lives can impact others, just as the events of history have shaped the world we live in today.

In sharing this story, I hope to inspire others to seek out the remnants of history in their own lives, to recognize the significance of their experiences, and to understand how they can contribute to the greater narrative of faith and service. Just as I found a piece of the past beneath the waves, may we all dive deep into our own journeys, uncovering the treasures of wisdom and purpose that lie beneath the surface.

As I continue to reflect on my experiences, both in the military and in my spiritual journey, I am reminded that every moment—every discovery— has the potential to lead us closer to understanding God's purpose for our lives. Just as the waters of Corregidor hold a piece of history, our lives are filled with opportunities to uncover the divine truth that God has placed within us.

In that home, I continued to nurture the spirit of hospitality and love that had always defined my life. It became a gathering place for friends and family, a space where we could share meals, laughter, and heartfelt conversations about our faith journeys. Knowing that a figure like General MacArthur had once enjoyed similar moments in that very room added a layer of significance to our gatherings, inspiring us to reflect on the impact we could have in our own spheres of influence.

As I transitioned from that beloved home in Eustis to my new life in The Villages, I carried with me the memories of both my time there and the echoes of history that resonated within those walls. The lessons learned and the connections made were not just personal milestones; they were part of a larger narrative that God was weaving throughout my life.

In sharing this story, I hope to inspire others to recognize the significance of their own homes and the legacies they can build within them. Just as General MacArthur found solace and inspiration in that Florida room, may we all create spaces where love, faith, and community can flourish, leaving behind a legacy that honors God and uplifts those around us.

I would always say to my wife, great men follow one another!

What a blessing it was to have crossed the path of such great men living and passing.

My four years in the Aggressor Squadron went by so fast, but it gave me the opportunity to study and learn enemy tactics and help teach our Blue forces how to counter and dominate the skies. The force of Satan is big and bad, but we have the ultimate weapons system, God; we just need to learn how to implement God's tactics to ensure our victory for eternity.

As I look back on that bold statement made during the Wednesday night Bible class, I recognize it as a pivotal moment in my spiritual journey—a calling that stirred deep within me. In response to that prompting, I felt compelled to prepare a sermon that I shared with several churches in the area.

The message was simple yet profound: we have an enemy, a very real adversary, that the Bible speaks about 142 times. Therefore, we must train ourselves to defeat that enemy and strive to become leaders—Top Guns for God.

As the calling grew stronger, I took the next step by developing a training program, inviting men to sign up for a year of Top Gun training. This program was designed to equip them with the spiritual tools and strategies necessary to confront the challenges we face as believers. The seed of this vision continued to grow, and I began to think about creating a curriculum that would cater to all ages, teaching them how to overcome the specific temptations that Satan targets at different stages of life.

I envisioned training children, teenagers, young adults, business leaders, politicians, athletes, coaches—people from every walk of life. The goal was to equip them to counter every tactic that Satan throws our way. I thought, "Wow, what a great world it would be if we were all Top Guns for God." Imagine a community of believers united in purpose and equipped to face the trials of life with unwavering faith.

While my official Top Gun training may be outdated and quite different from the modern Air Force, it provided a solid foundation for me to develop a concept tailored for the family of God. I couldn't begin to comprehend why God had sent me down this exciting path of life, but I trusted that He had a purpose in it all.

Like pilots who train to fly together and defeat their enemies, the spiritual parallel highlights the importance of uniting our spirits to create strength—much like the roots of a giant Sequoia tree. These trees stand tall and resilient, their roots intertwining to support one another against the fiercest storms. Similarly, we, as believers, must form a strong foundation of support for one another, creating a formidable pillar of strength to stand against Satan.

In the world of fighter pilots, the phrase "I got your six" signifies a commitment to watching out for one another, ensuring that no one is left vulnerable. This mentality is crucial for Christians as well; we must adopt the same daily mindset in our spiritual battles against the enemy. By standing together, encouraging one another, and holding each other accountable, we can navigate the challenges of faith with confidence and courage.

As I developed the training program and curriculum, I was filled with hope and excitement for the impact it could have on individuals and communities. My desire was to inspire a new generation of Top Guns for

God—warriors equipped to face the spiritual battles of their lives, ready to defend their faith and support one another in the process.

Through this journey, I have come to understand that God often leads us down paths we may not initially comprehend, but His plans are always greater than our own. As we strive to become Top Guns for God, may we remember the importance of unity, strength, and vigilance in our spiritual warfare. Together, we can create a legacy of faith that empowers others to join the fight against the darkness, standing firm in the light of God's truth.

Chapter 3

Training of an Air Weapons Controller

In the next few chapters, I will take you on a journey through my experiences as an Air Weapons Controller, shedding light on the critical role we play in aerial combat operations. You'll gain insight into the rigorous training that shaped my skills and prepared me for the challenges ahead.

As an Air Weapons Controller, my responsibilities extended far beyond simple coordination. I was tasked with managing air operations, guiding pilots in real-time, and making split-second decisions that could mean the difference between victory and defeat in the skies. This role required not only technical proficiency but also the ability to think strategically under pressure. I will share the intricacies of this position, illustrating how it is both an art and a science, demanding a deep understanding of tactics, communication, and teamwork.

You will also get a glimpse into my training—an intense and transformative experience that pushed me to my limits and honed my abilities. From the classroom to the simulation room, every moment was designed to prepare us for the complexities of aerial warfare. I will recount the challenges we faced, the lessons learned, and the camaraderie developed among my fellow trainees.

At the heart of this journey was a divine calling that led me to an extraordinary opportunity: the chance to attend and graduate from the elite Air Force Fighter Weapons School (FWS). This prestigious institution is known for producing the best of the best—those who would go on to lead and innovate in the realm of air combat. I will share how God guided me through this process, opening doors and providing blessings that I could never have anticipated.

As I reflect on my time at FWS, I recognize it not just as a pinnacle of military training but as a pivotal moment in my spiritual journey. The lessons learned there transcended the cockpit, shaping my understanding of leadership, faith, and the importance of serving others.

Join me as I delve into these experiences, revealing how they laid the groundwork for my calling to be a Top Gun for God. Through the lens of my military background, I hope to draw parallels that will encourage you to recognize the divine purpose in your own journey and to understand how God equips us for the battles we are called to fight.

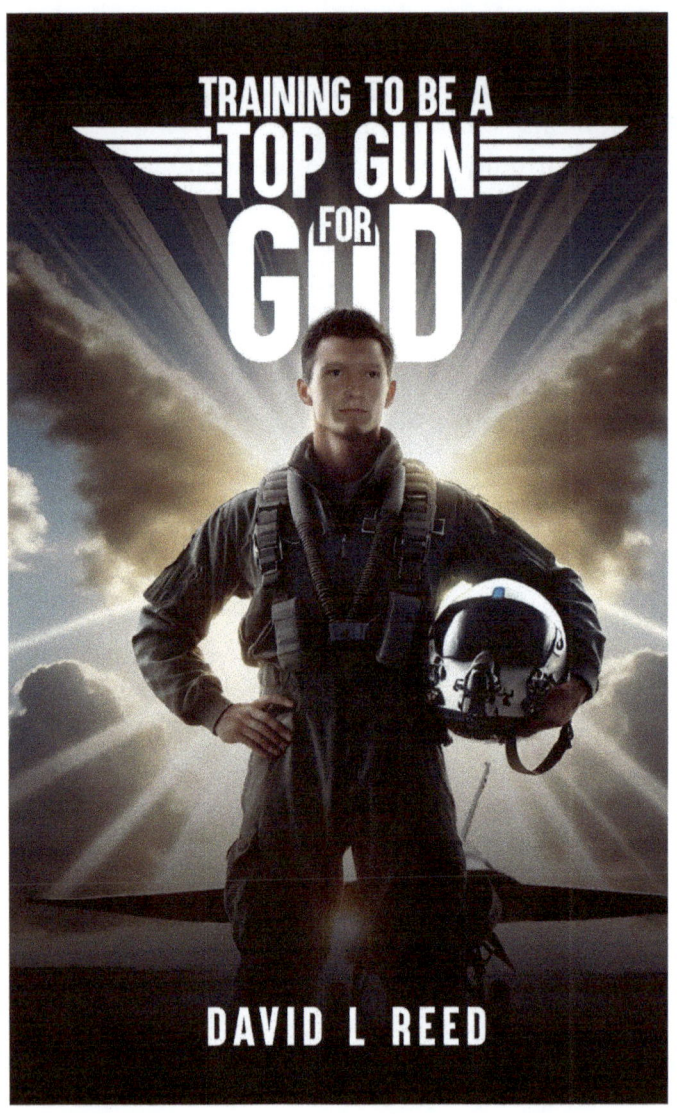

TRAINING TO BE A TOP GUN FOR GOD

DAVID L REED

My initial Air Weapons Controller training began at Tyndall Air Force Base in Panama City Beach, Florida, in 1978.

You might want to sit down as I prepare you for the exposure to this highly sensitive computerized system we use to obtain precise data for protecting our nation and killing the enemy.

I will show you one of the most sophisticated computers you will ever witness in your life, the "Wiz Wheel." I am sure God had a good laugh during our days of dependence upon this technology!

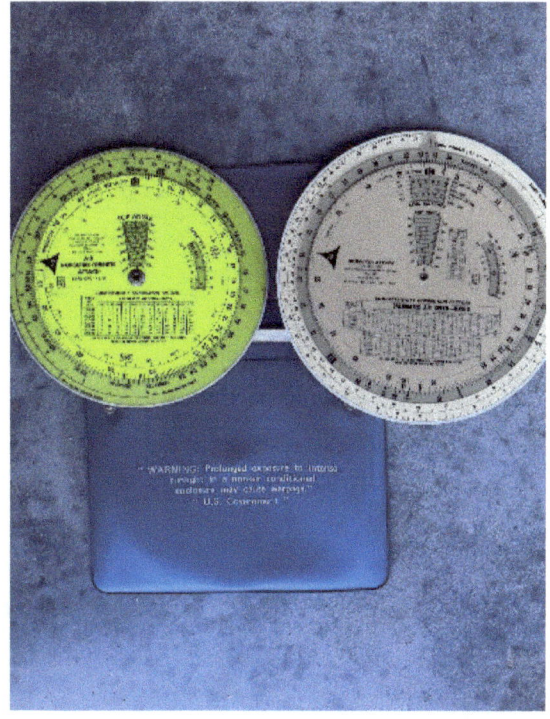

31

Surely, you were not expecting to see a sophisticated computer, and they did not come to market for a few years after this.

In the late 70s, without computers, we were operating under the old Air Defense Warfighting operations, and we had to be skilled in setting the direction, speed and altitude for completing an interception on an enemy aircraft. We were trained by this book and these two computers to compute as fast as humanly possible the attack parameters to ensure we got the kill.

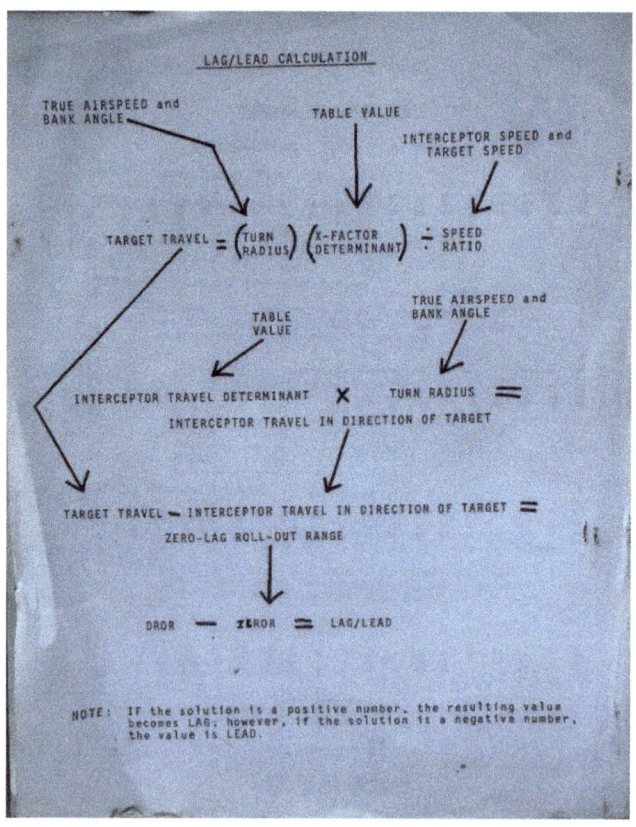

Trust me, it was a very challenging system to navigate, as the pilot's life rested in the hands of someone they hoped was exceptionally skilled at performing the necessary calculations. As an Air Weapons Controller, I was responsible for executing a range of manual calculations while simultaneously controlling the aircraft and orchestrating successful interceptions. The pressure was immense, as every decision I made could have serious implications for the mission and the lives of the pilots in the air.

These calculations were not trivial; they required a deep understanding of physics, geometry, and aerodynamics. I had to compute intercept courses, predict enemy movements, and assess various variables that could impact the mission. Each calculation was a vital piece of the puzzle, and mastering these high-tech manual computing skills was essential for ensuring the safety and effectiveness of our operations.

After honing these manual skills, my journey took me to Luke Air Force Base in Phoenix, Arizona, where I transitioned to learning about the 407L Semi-Automated System. This system represented a significant advancement, providing a semi-computerized tool designed to facilitate and expedite our interceptive vectors. The 407L offered a blend of human expertise and technological assistance, allowing us to enhance our operational efficiency while reducing the cognitive load on the controllers.

Graduating from the 407L Training at Luke Air Force Base was a proud moment for me. I felt equipped with the knowledge and skills to leverage this new technology effectively, merging the precision of manual calculations with the speed and accuracy of automated systems. This training laid the groundwork for my future assignments, enabling me to adapt to the evolving landscape of air combat.

Upon completing my training, I was assigned to the 728th Tactical Air Control Squadron at Eglin Air Force Base in Fort Walton Beach, Florida. This assignment was a significant step in my career, as it allowed me to put my training into practice and further develop my skills in a real-world setting. I spent two years there, immersing myself in the dynamics of air control and gaining invaluable experience in tactical operations.

During my time at Eglin, I learned the importance of teamwork and communication as we worked closely with pilots and other units to ensure mission success. The camaraderie developed within the squadron was a source of strength, and I cherished the relationships formed with my fellow controllers and pilots.

Ultimately, my dedication and performance led to my selection to join the Air Force Aggressors. This elite unit would allow me to take my skills to the next level, training U.S. and Allied forces in the art of aerial combat and preparing them for the challenges they would face. The journey from manual calculations to advanced systems was a testament to my growth and the divine guidance that led me to this point in my career.

As I reflect on this part of my journey, I recognize that each experience, each challenge, and each lesson learned was a crucial step in preparing me for the mission that lay ahead—not just in the military but in my spiritual calling to be a Top Gun for God.

Getting My Tactical Call Sign

Completing my training and arriving at Eglin AFB, Fort Walton Beach, Florida, was the beginning of my learning curve. I was in a whole new field, fresh out of school, but really excited to be working with the flying mission. I did not arrive with a Tactical Call Sign. That was coming soon.

In my present season of life, when someone addresses me by call sign, "Shadow," it brings back precious memories from my younger days and some of the most exhilarating times in my life as an Air Weapons Controller in the U.S. Air Force.

Like many Controllers and Pilots, when you arrive at your first assignment, the members of the squadron often notice something distinctive about you or a particular action that sparks a playful thought in their minds, leading to the creation of your call sign. For me, this happened during my first assignment at Duke Field, an Auxiliary Base of Eglin AFB in Fort Walton Beach, Florida.

I was sitting in a crowded office that had eight controllers squeezed into a very small office space. I had my feet propped, and I threw a ball of paper across the room into a trash can (yes, I made it). A senior Second Lieutenant (call sign Spade) saw the action and said I reminded him of that guy on TV, the White Shadow. So, he gave me that name, and it became my Tactical Call Sign, but I had to shorten it down for brevity's sake, so I became known as "Shadow."

My time at Duke provided me with essential insights into strategy, teamwork, and the significance of making swift decisions under pressure. As I went through rigorous training and participated in real-world missions, I started to recognize the similarities between the discipline demanded in the military and the spiritual readiness needed for a faithful life. Still clueless about how God was preparing me for this book.

To nurture my faith, I ensured that my family remained actively engaged with the Niceville Church of Christ. I led the youth program and played a key role in establishing a sponsorship program aimed at fostering connections across generations, encouraging members of the church to engage with and support the younger generation. My dear friends Lynn and Travis Griffin took over the program and kept it going for many years.

In the cockpit, pilots rely on their training to confront tangible threats. Similarly, Christians must equip themselves with knowledge and prayer to confront the spiritual challenges that arise in daily life. Just as pilots undergo rigorous training to become proficient in their craft, believers must engage in spiritual disciplines to become effective warriors for God.

Reflecting on my early days, I recall the steep learning curve I faced while working alongside some of the best pilots in the Air Force. Even though I was not a pilot, because I was an integral part of the flying mission, I was put on Flying Status, which meant I could fly when time permitted and a seat was available.

The excitement of being part of the flying mission and a team dedicated to excellence was palpable, but so was the pressure to perform at a high level.

I encountered challenges that tested my resolve and commitment. Each day brought new opportunities to learn, grow, and develop my skills. The mentorship I received from military and seasoned spiritual leaders was instrumental in shaping my understanding of leadership and the importance of humility.

In my early days, I had the pleasure of controlling a lot of experienced war pilots who were excited to be flying our new F-15 Fighting Eagles. My learning curve was pretty steep, learning airplanes, pilot strengths, and my own skills and shortfalls, but I advanced quickly in my field and developed a great rapport with the pilots.

I loved my new career; it was a very exciting and rewarding field for this old country boy! I did not know how rewarding it was going to be, but God did.

Most of the guys I worked with did not know my name; they just knew me by my Tactical Call Sign "Shadow." That is how they would address me during our missions.

I loved my job as I would wake up at 4:00 am excited to go to the F-15 Squadron for a 5:00 am pre-mission briefing. Usually, it would be me and sometimes another controller meeting with 4 F-15 pilots planning our morning training mission. One of us would control two of the four that would be Blue Forces, and the other would control the other two that played the role of Red Forces. As soon as the briefing was over, we would drive 18 miles to Duke Field, where our unit was located, and we would get ready to control our mission.

By going early for the face-to-face briefings, I developed a great rapport with my pilots. Some controllers skipped the face-to-face and would just do a phone pre-brief. I was very consistent in attending the face-to-face briefings, as I loved the team spirit and the immediate feedback for my own improvement.

In January 1979-80 time frame, the 33rd Tactical Fighter Wing was invited to deploy to their first Red Flag Exercise in the F-15; I was elated when they invited "Shadow" to go and be their Controller.

Once we arrived at Nellis AFB, Nevada, it was so exciting to see all of the jets on the flight line. Units came from all over the country, including Allied Nations. On the first flight across the Nellis Range, the squadron Operations Officer, Lt Colonel Neely Johnson, Tactical Call Sign, "Kingfish," asked me if I wanted to go for a ride. Needless to say, I was so excited I said yes!

Strapping into the back seat of the F15 and taking off for the first time was the most exciting moment of my life. It was such a thrill. Kingfish was great, as he warned me before we did our first high "G" turn. We did a 6 "G" turn, and it was so cool feeling my body experiencing the tightest hug of my life. I was learning what my pilots would be experiencing during a high "G" turn when they would be in a dogfight.

He also gave me the stick to let me fly the F15 and allowed me, for just a moment, to change my role from being a controller to actually flying the F-15 Eagle. I had the pleasure of flying many times after that, but that first ride was a memory I will always cherish.

When the Red Flag Exercise started, for the first time, I was controlling in a real war-sized environment; it was so different from the small missions we ran back home. There were airplanes everywhere. All kinds of planes executed many kinds of missions, which made my job harder than I could ever have imagined. It was like war! Just like it was supposed to be. This was my first Red Flag, and I loved it. I also realized in life, we are in a Red Flag exercise every day in our fight against Satan. We are given a warning in I Peter:

1 Peter 5:8: "Be alert and of sober mind. Your enemy, the devil, prowls around like a roaring lion, looking for someone to devour."

It was truly a rewarding experience, a moment that allowed "Shadow" to prove his mettle on the battlefield of aerial combat. As an Air Weapons Controller, I had trained rigorously to develop the skills necessary to guide pilots through the complexities of air engagements. The opportunity to showcase those skills came near the end of the Red Flag exercise, a premier training event designed to simulate real combat scenarios and test the limits of our tactical capabilities.

During this intense exercise, I was approached by several F-106 Delta Dart Interceptor pilots. They sought my expertise, asking me to control them against the formidable F-15s—new super fighters that were known for their agility and advanced technology. It was a humbling moment, as these experienced pilots recognized the value of my insights and were eager to learn how to effectively engage the enemy.

With a sense of pride and responsibility, I shared a few tips and provided tactical guidance that I believed would give them an edge in the upcoming engagement. I emphasized the importance of situational awareness, the need to leverage the Delta Dart's strengths, and how to exploit the vulnerabilities of the F-15s. It was a collaborative effort, and I felt a deep sense of camaraderie with these pilots as we worked together to strategize our approach.

As the exercise unfolded, I watched with anticipation as the Delta Darts took to the skies under my direction. The tension was palpable, and I could feel the weight of the moment. Then, to my exhilaration, the Delta Darts achieved their first kill on the F-15s. The thrill of that success resonated deeply within me; it was a testament to the effectiveness of our teamwork and the tactical guidance I had provided.

At that moment, the skills behind the Call Sign "Shadow" were making their mark on the Red Flag battlefield. I felt a sense of fulfillment, knowing that I had contributed to the success of the mission and played a role in empowering those pilots to achieve their objectives. It was more than just a personal victory; it was a validation of the training and dedication that had brought me to this point in my career.

This experience reinforced my belief in the importance of collaboration and the value of sharing knowledge. Just as I had guided those pilots, I realized that my journey was leading me toward a greater calling—one that would involve equipping and inspiring others in their own battles, both in the air and in their spiritual lives.

Reflecting on that day, I understood that the lessons learned on the Red Flag battlefield extended far beyond military tactics. They served as a reminder of the power of teamwork, the significance of mentorship, and the impact we can have on one another's journeys. As I moved forward in my career, I carried those lessons with me, ready to embrace the next chapter of my life as both a warrior in the skies and a Top Gun for God.

Mentorship and Leadership

Mentorship plays a vital role in both military and spiritual journeys. Throughout my career, I had the privilege of learning from exceptional leaders who not only imparted their knowledge but also embodied integrity and dedication. Their guidance enabled me to navigate the complexities of my role and inspired me to strive for excellence. Yet, the most significant excellence we can pursue is our understanding of God's Word and His strategies for confronting Satan's tactics. Imagine yourself as a leader teaching other souls how to defeat Satan; you must envision it and yearn for it to make it a reality.

In the context of faith, mentorship can take many forms—whether it's through a pastor, a spiritual mentor, or a trusted friend. These relationships provide encouragement, accountability, and wisdom as we seek to grow in our faith. Back to the Red Flag, Initially, I was a Blue Forces Controller, and my role was to provide "close control" for our fighter aircraft when they were demonstrating real-time counter tactics against the Red Force enemy tactics.

I will give you a peek in the following photo of what we saw on our scope. The Red and Blue Arrows would not be on our scope, and they are input here to help my readers get a better picture of what is happening. All I had to work with was the small radar returns.

When you look at the drawing below you can see that after a merged plot it was difficult to know Red from Blue Forces. It was not an easy task, especially when the skies are filled with aircraft, unlike this simple 4 vs 4 training scenario.

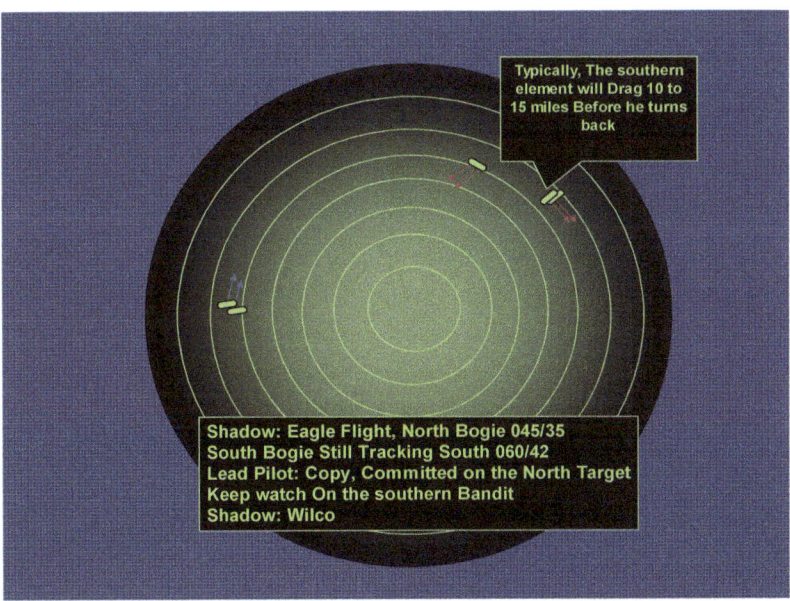

When I later joined the Aggressor Squadron, I would be the one controlling the Red Forces and running enemy tactics.

When the pilots would check into my airspace and we were ready to execute our training scenario I would give a call to both sides, "Fights

On". That indicates all players are in the Military Operating Area (MOA) airspace that we can safely start the training mission.

"Fights On", is also a call for Christians to make with they perceive Satan has entered their "air/life space". When we sense Satan creeping into our space, we need to alert one another with a "check six" or a "Fights On" call, indicating we have spotted the enemy, so initiate counter tactics (we will discuss some of those tactics later in the book).

Going back to my control procedures, my typical dialogue between me and the pilot of my Baron Flight, during Air-to-Air combat training mission, would sound something like this:

Shadow: Baron Flight, 2 contacts, 220/35/18K

Pilot: Shadow, Baron One, contact 220/35/18K.

Shadow: contact bandit, kill.

Baron One: copy Kill.

At a certain range I would implement our split tactics to confuse the Blue Forces.

Baron One: Shadow Baron One Engaged

Shadow: Copy engaged, spitter NW 22K, Left turn

Baron One: Copy, Tally

The closer the pilot (Red or Blue) gets to the heat of the battle, the more critical his training becomes. If his training is lacking refined skills, he most likely loses the battle and dies.

In our faith journey, believers are called to recognize that they are engaged in a battle that transcends the physical realm. This battle is not against flesh and blood but against spiritual forces that seek to undermine our relationship with God.

The concept of being a "Top Gun for God" encapsulates the idea of stepping into this spiritual warfare with courage, dedication, and a commitment to victory.

God mentions Satan, Devil, and Evil One, 142 times in the Bible and 65 times in the New Testament. That should be a great "Heads Up" call that Satan is very real.

Spiritual Enemy Defined

Satan is often referred to as the father of lies, and he is the adversary we must contend with. His tactics include deception, temptation, and accusation, all aimed at leading believers astray. The 142 Scriptures that mention the evil one provides insight into his character and strategies. They remind us of the need to be vigilant and discerning. Recognizing these tactics is a critical first step in overcoming them. Look at how the Apostle John describes Satan.

John 8:44: "You belong to your father, the devil, and you want to carry out your father's desires. He was a murderer from the beginning, not holding to the truth, for there is no truth in him. When he lies, he speaks his native language, for he is a liar and the father of lies."

Call to Action

As we embark on this journey together, I encourage you to embrace your role as a spiritual warrior. Equip yourself with the tools necessary for victory—prayer, Scripture, and a community of believers. Together, we can engage in this battle, knowing that through Christ, we have the power to overcome.

Reflection Questions

What does being a "Top Gun" for God mean to you personally?

In what ways have you experienced spiritual warfare in your own life?

How can you prepare yourself for the battles you face in your faith journey.

Chapter 4

Fighter Weapons School

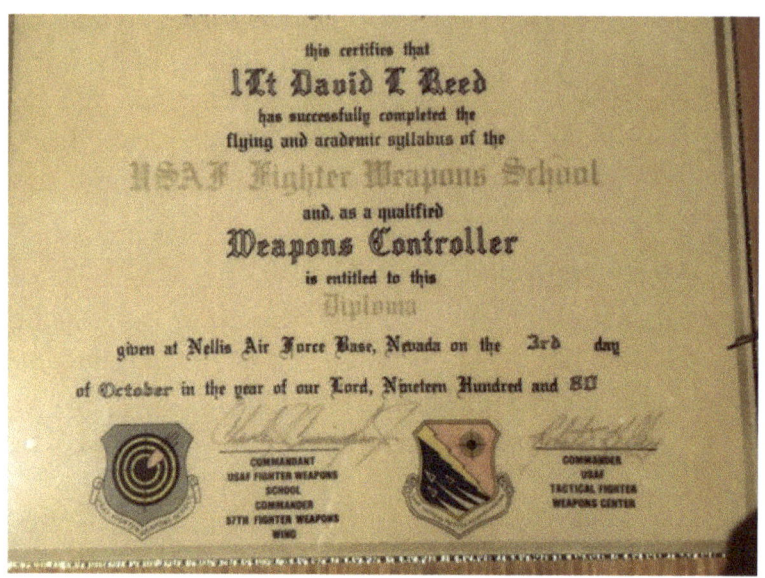

Weapons School Class 80 Ban

The U.S. Air Force Weapons School has always stood as a testament to the rigorous training that pilots weapons controllers undergo to prepare for combat. Its history traces back to the Aircraft Gunnery School established in 1949 at Las Vegas Air Force Base. The base was renamed to Nellis Air Force Base in 1950. In January 1954, the school assumed the mission of training fighter instructors and took on the name "USAF Fighter Weapons School."

The school trained pilots in the P-51 Mustang, F-80 Shooting Star, F-84 Thunderjet, and, in the 1960s, the F-100 and F-105 Thunderchief. In 1965, during the Vietnam era, they added the F-4 Phantom II to their courses.

In the post-Vietnam era, a whole new fighting force was added, including the F-15s, A-10, F-4D, Aggressor Division F-5E, and F-16C.

In the early 1970s the Aggressors were added, flying the T-38 Talon and the F-5E Tiger II, providing accurate threat replication for dissimilar air combat tactics (DACT). The Aggressors were formed in 1975. In 1977, the A-10 Thunderbolt II and the F-15 Eagle were added to the school.

Since my class graduated in 1980, the school has gone through many changes in its structure and its mission. I won't bore you with all the changes since they came after my graduation date, I will speak to my own personal experiences. The Air Weapons Controller Division, later known as the Command and Control Division, was activated as a separate unit in 1987.

Weapons School Graduates of this esteemed program are not just pilots; they are tactical experts equipped to lead and mentor others. The training is intense, requiring candidates to demonstrate exceptional skills in mission planning, execution, and leadership. This level of preparation is essential for success in the high-stakes environment of air combat.

After two years of proving my mettle at Eglin, I was blessed to be selected to join the Air Force Aggressor Squadron. The Air Force only had four Aggressor Squadrons to train all our US and Allied Forces around the globe.

This was my Enemy Weapons School graduating Class, October 3, 1980. That is me standing on the far-left side. There were two pilots and three Weapons Controllers from this class that went to the Pacific team. Other members of my class stayed at Nellis; some went to Europe.

There were two squadrons at Nellis AFB, NV, for training all US Forces, one in the Pacific and one in Europe. The Fighter Weapons School, located at Nellis AFB, Nevada, trained all of the pilots and Air Weapons Controllers assigned to these units.

After graduating from FWS, I attended another Soviet Awareness course in Washington DC. I can only say it was great because it was a highly classified course on our enemy forces. It was God's way of opening new doors for the vision he had planned for my future.

I still remember getting off the plane at Clark AB November 1980, and having members of my new squadron there to greet us and help us get to the base hotel. The squadron was located at Clark AB, Philippines. We had around 20 pilots and 8 Air Weapons Controllers.

It was a very busy lifestyle as we would travel to all of the US Bases and Allied Nations (Blue Forces) in the Pacific theater and conduct training for defeating enemy's tactics (Red Forces) for two weeks, followed by two weeks at home to catch up on our paperwork!

Lessons for Spiritual Growth

The principles learned in all military training can be directly applied to spiritual growth. Just as pilots must develop discipline, perseverance, and teamwork, Christians are called to cultivate these same qualities in their faith journey.

Consider the importance of discipline: just as pilots adhere to strict protocols, believers must commit to spiritual disciplines such as prayer, Bible study, and worship. These practices not only deepen our relationship with God but also prepare us to face the challenges that lie ahead.

Real-World Applications

Throughout Scripture, we see examples of individuals who faced spiritual battles with courage and faith. David, for instance, faced Goliath not only with a slingshot but with the confidence that God was with him. Similarly, we are called to confront our own giants with the assurance that God equips us for victory.

1 Corinthians 9:25: "Everyone who competes in the games goes into strict training. They do it to get a crown that will not last, but we do it to get a crown that will last forever."

Expanding on Military Strategies

Military strategies often involve understanding the terrain, anticipating the enemy's moves, and preparing for various scenarios. In our spiritual lives, we must also be aware of the "terrain" we navigate—our environments, influences, and the people we interact with. The highly educated seek knowledge to sustain their positions as truth seekers, but they often overlook those giant words that proceed with the core of the information they support. Words like "if this happens" are often overlooked making everything that follows purely speculative information to stir the emotions of the weaker, less Godly guided, spirits.

Understanding the Terrain: Just as pilots study maps and flight paths, Christians must understand the world around them. This includes recognizing cultural influences that may lead us away from God's truth.

Anticipating Attacks:

Just as a pilot anticipates enemy actions, we must be vigilant against temptations and spiritual attacks. This requires prayerful discernment and a deep understanding of Scripture. God's word is your weapon.

Hebrews 4:12: "For the word of God is alive and active. Sharper than any double-edged sword, it penetrates even dividing soul and spirit, joints and marrow; it judges the thoughts and attitudes of the heart."

No other weapon compares to this power.

Preparing for Various Scenarios:

In military training, pilots prepare for different combat scenarios. Similarly, Christians should equip themselves with knowledge of biblical truths to respond to various life situations with wisdom and grace.

When does the Top Gun training start? According to God, he sees the training of the spirit should start when a child is very young.

Proverbs 22:6: "Start children off on the way they should go, and even when they are old, they will not turn from it."

Reflection Questions

How can you apply the principles of military training to your spiritual growth?

What specific disciplines do you need to incorporate into your daily routine?

How can you better understand the spiritual terrain in which you live and work?

Chapter 5

Life in a Top Gun Squadron

HAVE MIG-WILL TRAVEL

DAVE "SHADOW" REED
AGGRESSOR CONTROLLER

26 TFTAS
45120/46112

PSC No. 1 Box 2999
APO S.F. 96286

We had cool cards and cars!!!

Living life in the fast lane was not just a saying; it was a lesson we embraced wholeheartedly in the Aggressor Squadron. Our missions took us across the vast expanse of the Pacific theater, giving us ample road time to travel and engage in advanced training exercises. This unique opportunity allowed me to further hone my skills, immersing myself in a variety of roles that simulated multiple threat scenarios.

The experience was both challenging and incredibly rewarding. I learned to adopt the tactics of our adversaries, simulating enemy maneuvers and strategies with precision. This training was not just about honing my own skills; it was about preparing U.S. and Allied Nation pilots to respond effectively to the challenges they might face in combat. The responsibility weighed heavily on us, but the knowledge that we were contributing to the safety and readiness of our forces made every effort worthwhile.

Our Aggressor Squadron was assigned to the 3rd Tactical Fighter Wing at Clark Air Base in the Philippines. Arriving at Clark with my family in November 1980 marked the beginning of a whole new adventure—a significant learning curve not just in my military career but in my personal life as well. The vibrant culture, the stunning landscapes, and the camaraderie of my fellow service members made for an unforgettable experience.

I often reflect on how God was directing my steps down a road that few men could only imagine. The blessings I received during this time were abundant, and I still feel incredibly grateful for the honor of serving in such a prestigious unit. It was a time of growth, both professionally and spiritually, as I navigated the challenges of military life while deepening my faith.

As a parting gift when leaving the squadron, each member received a photo signed by their comrades—a tangible record of the memories we shared together. This photo was more than just an image; it was a representation of the bonds we formed, the experiences we endured, and the laughter we shared. Each signature told a story, encapsulating the spirit of teamwork and the friendships that transcended our roles as service members.

In looking back at that time, I am reminded of the lessons learned and the relationships built. The Aggressor Squadron was not just a unit; it was a family. We were united in our mission and dedicated to one another, embodying the essence of what it means to be part of something greater than ourselves.

As I continue on my journey, I carry those memories with me, using them as a foundation for my calling to inspire others in their own battles—whether in the skies or in their spiritual lives. The experiences I gained at Clark Air Base have shaped who I am today, and I remain committed to sharing the lessons learned with those who seek to become Top Guns for God.

The signatures surrounding the photo of our F-5 flight formation belong to future leaders destined for remarkable careers in the Air Force. Some went on to become astronauts four-star generals, and held various high-ranking positions, including Vice Chief of Staff of the United States Air Force and Commander of Combat Air Command.

If you look closely, you'll notice one individual signed it twice: Mark Polansky, known as "Jet Eye" and later as "Roman." He became an astronaut and flew on three shuttle missions, including serving as the Commander of the Space Shuttle Endeavour, which launched with a crew of seven astronauts. The shuttle lifted off from NASA Kennedy Space Center's Launch Pad 39A at 6:03 p.m. EDT on Wednesday, July 15, 2009.

STS-127 Mission Facts:

Mission: Deliver and install components of the Japanese Experiment Module

Space Shuttle: Endeavour

Launch Pad: 39A

Launch Date: July 15, 2009, at 6:03 p.m. EDT

Landing Site: Kennedy Space Center, Florida

Landing Date: July 31, 2009, at 10:48 a.m. EDT

Mission Duration: 15 days, 16 hours, 44 minutes, and 58 seconds

Inclination/Altitude: 51.6 degrees/122 nautical miles

Miles Traveled: 6.5 million

What Mark was unaware of was that on that evening, one of his former Aggressor Controllers was hosting a Bible study at his residence in Eustis, Florida. The gathering took place on his private dock by Lake Louise, where the group came together to watch the launch and offer prayers for Mark's safe journey through space and his eventual return. It was genuinely a privilege to pray for my fellow Aggressor, "Jet Eye."

Meeting Lt General Thomas McInerney

Another highlight of my Air Force career was having the privilege to meet and serve under the 3rd Tactical Fighter Wing Commander, Colonel Thomas McInerney, who later became a Lt General, the Vice Chief of Staff USAF, and a Fox News Contributor for many years.

In the photo above, Colonel McInerney is seen pinning an Accommodation Medal on the very young 1st Lieutenant David Reed. Our Aggressor Squadron fell under his command, and he was by far the best Wing Commander I had the pleasure of serving under in my 22-year Air Force career.

I did not fully appreciate at the time what a great warfighting tactician Colonel McInerney was, but he was soon to prove his mettle.

After being selected for his promotion to Brigadier General Officer, he moved to Kadena AFB, in Okinawa, and took over 313 Air Division that included all of the F-15 Fighting Eagle Squadrons that previously had F-4 Phantoms.

As we would deploy there to train the F-15 pilots, it was an honor to witness how General Mac was expanding the warfighting skills of all the flying forces at Kadena from a 2 man fighting element to a four ship killing machine, and he had the entire Pacific Theater trained to fly in even greater formations.

Known affectionately, and referred to as "General Mac," he was not only a brilliant tactician but also a leader who genuinely cared for those under his command. His vision and expertise were instrumental in improving the F-15 warfighting skills for the United States Air Force.

One of his most significant achievements was executing the first F-15 Large Theater Force Employment Exercise (LTFEE) in Air Force history, a groundbreaking event that would shape future military operations.

I had the privilege of controlling that first LTFEE, an exercise designed to demonstrate how to end wars quickly and effectively. It is a memory I will never forget. My deployment from Clark Air Base in the Philippines took me to a mountaintop radar site in South Korea known as Blue Boy. From my vantage point, I was tasked with monitoring my four F-5 Combat Air Patrol (CAP) fighters, eagerly waiting for the action to commence.

As I sat on scope, I noticed something unusual to the southwest—a massive cloud, possibly a large chaff drop, shaped like a big banana. A chaff drop involves the release of chaff, a material used in military operations to confuse or deceive radar and infrared-guided missiles. Typically made up of small strips or fibers of aluminum or other reflective materials, chaff creates false targets on radar screens, enhancing the survivability of aircraft by making it difficult for adversaries to lock onto them.

I measured the cloud to be over 20 miles in length and at an altitude of about 22,000 feet. It remained intact for several sweeps on my scope, drifting northward. Then, suddenly, I watched in disbelief as it began to break up. It dawned on me that this was not chaff but rather a massive number of aircraft that had just divided to implement a large pincer attack on the entire peninsula of South Korea.

A wave of helplessness washed over me. I was acutely aware that this was a training exercise, but the scenario felt all too real. If it had been an actual attack, I would have been telling my pilots goodbye as they faced overwhelming odds. The outnumbered F-5s would have been at a severe disadvantage, and I would likely have become an early target, as radar sites were always high-priority targets in the initial phases of an assault.

I wish I could share more details about the mission outcome, but it was highly sensitive, and as the saying goes, if I told you, I would have to shoot you! Nevertheless, I still remember thinking, "Great job, General Mac!" His tactical genius, which I had witnessed firsthand, was implemented in the first Gulf War and played a significant role in why that conflict only lasted 42 days.

Reflecting on those experiences, I realize the profound impact that leaders like General McInerney have on their teams and the broader mission. His ability to innovate and inspire was a driving force behind our success, and I carry those lessons with me as I continue my journey, both in military service and in my spiritual calling as a Top Gun for God.

When all of my days ended with the Aggressors, I realized I was passing through what would be a true highlight of my life. I loved all the guys we had the pleasure to serve with, even the ones that would buzz my radar van or my Jeep when I was positioned on a mountain side with binoculars watching for the low-level ingress of F-16s into Cro Valley in the Philippines.

We had great deployments all over the Pacific theater and lots of fun parties when we got back home. I never envisioned when I became an officer that I would ever get to be in a squadron with so many great men. I was truly blessed.

Formal

InFormal

Chapter 6

William Tell 1982

My training was not over; God had more things for me to learn. I never knew I would be telling these stories 43 years later, but God did.

Many of the F-15 guys I had controlled at Eglin had transitioned to the Pacific Theater to the 18 Tactical Fighter Wing, Kadena Air Force Base, Okinawa.

In the summer of 1982, the Pacific Forces at Kadena were assigned the privilege for being one of the first F-15 Squadrons to compete in the 1982 William Tell Air-to-Air Weapons Meet. This is a competition where all of the Top Pilots and Controllers come to compete to see who the best of the best worldwide – our Olympics.

Lt Colonel Jere Wallace, "Waldo," was assigned as the Team Leader. I had worked with "Waldo" at Eglin Air Force Base in Florida, and he asked me to lead the Weapons Control duties for the Pacific Team. Wow, this was the Super Bowl of the Air Force. I was so excited to be picked to be the Team Leader for the three-man Control Team.

My Commander approved my release, and I was on my way to the prestigious US and Allied Forces competition held in October 1982, at Tyndall Air Force Base in Florida.

We trained hard for 2 months to be ready to compete for four different profiles. All US and Allied Forces pilots and controllers from all around the globe were challenged to compete for the honor of being the best of the best and having their team's name engraved on the William Tell Trophy.

This competition tested the skills of fighter crews in air-to-air combat scenarios and was a showcase of aerial gunnery, tactics, and overall combat proficiency.

In the end of the 1982 William Tell competition, the Pacific Pilot Team, led by Lt Colonel Jere Wallace from the 18th Tactical Fighter Wing (18 TFW), along with the Weapons Control Team led by Captain David Reed, 26th Aggressor Squadron, were indeed the winners.

This competition highlighted the skill and coordination of both the aircrews and the supporting weapons control teams, emphasizing the importance of teamwork in achieving air superiority.

Did I ever have a dream of winning William Tell and being considered the best in the U.S. Air Force? No, but God did.

He wanted me to have that experience not for bragging rights but only to show everyone reading this book that even the life experiences of a High School dropout, poor boy from Kentucky, can be used to lead others to the top of a Worldwide Air to Air Competition. So don't let Satan tell you that you can't be a Top Gun for God because that is a LIE!!!

My focus in life today is to rise to the top of the spiritual pyramid and be the best Top Gun for God that I can be. With God as my Team Leader, I can achieve more than I could ever imagine.

Our spiritual likeness to God is not about our achievements; it is about what God achieves through us by spreading His invisible, powerful love into the world to defeat Satan's evil tactics intended to destroy God's family.

This achievement marked a significant turning point in my career, reinforcing the idea that God's guidance is present in every step of our journey. It reminded me that no matter what our background or past mistakes, we can achieve greatness through faith and dedication.

After William Tell in the spring of 1984, I was offered a staff job at the 13th Air Force, still at Clark AB, as the Standardization and Evaluation Officer, the Briefing Officer for the 13th Air Force Commander, and Chairman of the Regional Air Defense Network for all of the ASEAN Nations.

So, I had to hang up my flight suit and adorn my regular Air Force Blues and manage a desk and a staff of three. Trust me, in those days, that was a very difficult transition. Back in those days, prior to computers and PowerPoint, posting changes to the General's briefing was a two-day process, just to change one 35mm slide in the presentation.

We had a small church in Angeles City where we placed membership and was very involved in serving and helping to lead during our four and a half years there. That was another great memory that I still cherish today. We did not have a full-time pastor so all of the men would take turns doing the preaching. I always kept a sermon prepared in my Bible as occasionally, the guy scheduled to preach would be sick or have an unannounced TDY to another base.

Each year, our church hosted the FILAM lectureships, where missionaries from all around the Philippines would come for spiritual nourishment. Some years we would have men come from the US to lead the studies.

Our home always served as a free hotel for as many as five to ten visitors. We sometimes would offer our house to visitors even when we were gone.

59

The love of God was always an outpouring from the Reed household of hospitality.

DAVE "SHADOW" REED
AGGRESSOR
NOV 80 — MAR 84

This ink drawing captures the essence of my family and the great memories of working in the Top Gun Squadron for four years. It was truly an incredible gift that God bestowed upon the path of life. Through my experiences there, God planted the seed for this of defeating the enemy for this book. He led me to a Top Gun Squadron, where I experienced exceptional teamwork, joy, faith, and a great sense of family. Those four wonderful years were filled with unforgettable moments, including fun scuba diving, golfing, and hosting many missionaries in our home. I was learning the importance of giving out God's love to all.

Lessons Learned

Embrace Challenges:

Each challenge is an opportunity for growth. Embrace them with a positive attitude and a willingness to learn.

Seek Guidance: Don't hesitate to seek mentorship and guidance from those who have walked the path before you.

Stay Humble: No matter how much you achieve, always remember the importance of humility and gratitude toward God.

Reflection Questions

Who are the mentors in your life, and how have they influenced your journey?

What challenges have you faced that have led to significant growth?

How can you foster a spirit of humility amidst your achievements?

Chapter 7

Combat Spiritual Training

Role and Responsibilities

My role in our Air Force combat mission was the Air Weapons Controllers (AWCs) or the Air Battle Manager (ABM). Since most are not familiar with this role, I will try to elevate your understanding of the importance we played in the Air War. I use the past tense word "played" because our weapons systems have greatly advanced since my days, but my life experiences from the way we trained in the 70s-80s are reflected here, even though they might be greatly outdated.

Air Weapons Controllers (AWCs) played a critical role in managing air combat operations. They serve as the command-and-control element, providing essential support to pilots by ensuring they have the situational awareness needed to navigate complex battle environments.

AWCs were responsible for coordinating the actions of multiple aircraft, guiding them to engage targets and avoid threats. This requires not only technical expertise but also the ability to make quick decisions under pressure. They operate advanced radar systems and communicate vital information to pilots in real-time, ensuring mission success.

Importance of Communication

Effective communication is paramount in both military operations and spiritual contexts. In the heat of battle, clear and concise communication can mean the difference between victory and defeat. Similarly, in our spiritual lives, the ability to communicate with God through prayer and to support one another within the body of Christ is essential.

Consider how AWCs relay critical information to pilots. They provide updates on enemy positions, changes in mission parameters, and rules of engagement. In our spiritual lives, we must also seek to communicate openly with God, asking for guidance and clarity as we navigate our daily challenges.

Matthew 6:33: "But seek first the kingdom of God and His righteousness, and all these things shall be added to you."

Everything you need is there for the asking if you are an honest seeker of truth.

Team Dynamics

The dynamics of teamwork among AWCs and pilots are crucial for success. Just as AWCs must work seamlessly with pilots to execute missions, Christians are called to collaborate with one another in their faith journeys.

This collaboration involves encouraging one another, sharing burdens, and celebrating victories. By fostering a spirit of teamwork, believers can strengthen their resolve and enhance their effectiveness in spiritual warfare

Practical Application of AWC Principles

Situational Awareness: Just as AWCs maintain situational awareness, Christians must remain alert to the spiritual environment around them. This involves being mindful of influences that may lead us astray.

Coordination and Support:

AWCs coordinate actions among multiple aircraft, and similarly, Christians should work together to support one another in their faith. This can include prayer partnerships, accountability groups, and community outreach.

Real-Time Decision Making:

In combat, AWCs must make quick decisions based on available information. In our spiritual lives, we must also be prepared to respond to situations with wisdom and discernment, relying on the Holy Spirit for guidance

Reflection Questions

How can you improve your communication with God and others in your spiritual journey?

In what ways can you foster teamwork within your church or community?

Are there areas where you need to enhance your situational awareness spiritually?

Chapter 8

Full Armor of God

In the next four chapters, we will cover some general guidelines of Top Gun preparedness, followed by six chapters of Satan tactics and Top Gun countertactics.

The last two chapters will give guidance to help you see how God is leading you through special moments in life where He is creating God Stories to accomplish His purposes, and tell you all about your love basket God has made for you.

Pilots don't go to battle without their full armor, neither should you. When fighting our spiritual battles against our enemy, Satan, we need to be fully armed. So that means we put on the Full Armor of God every day. God describes it for us in **Ephesians 6:10-18.**

Ephesians 6:10: *"Finally, be strong in the Lord and in his mighty power."*

Ephesians 6:11: *"Put on the full armor of God, so that you can take your stand against the devil's schemes."*

Ephesians 6:12: *"For our struggle is not against flesh and blood, but against the rulers, against the authorities, against the powers of this dark world and against the spiritual forces of evil in the heavenly realms."*

Ephesians 6:13: *"Therefore put on the full armor of God, so that when the day of evil comes, you may be able to stand your ground, and after you have done everything, to stand."*

Ephesians 6:14: *"Stand firm then, with the belt of truth buckled around your waist, with the breastplate of righteousness in place,"*

Ephesians 6:15: *"and with your feet fitted with the readiness that comes from the gospel of peace."*

Ephesians 6:16: *"In addition to all this, take up the shield of faith, with which you can extinguish all the flaming arrows of the evil one."*

Ephesians 6:17: *"Take the helmet of salvation and the sword of the Spirit, which is the word of God."*

Ephesians 6:18: *"And pray in the Spirit on all occasions with all kinds of prayers and requests."*

Pilots don't go to their jet and forget their 'G' suit, or their helmet, or their flight boots, they go to battle fully armed. We need to be fully armed "every day" with our spiritual battle armor. God will be our endless fuel source and our superior weapons system, his truths, that assures us victory in the end.

God's Sovereignty

Understanding God's sovereignty is essential for believers, especially in times of trial. God is not only all-powerful but also intimately involved in our lives. His plans for us are good, and He works all things together for our benefit, even when we cannot see it.

Scripture provides reassurance that God's authority surpasses any challenge we may face. In **Romans 8:28**, we are reminded that "In all things God works for the good of those who love him." This promise serves as a foundation for our faith, encouraging us to trust in His ultimate plan. Keep in mind, it was 45 years ago His plan for this book began in my life, but it was planned by Him, before then.

Satan's Limitations

While Satan may exert influence and temptation, his power is limited. He cannot act without God's permission, and his attempts to derail believers are ultimately futile. The Bible reminds us that Jesus has already secured victory over sin and death through His resurrection.

Understanding Satan's limitations empowers believers to stand firm in their faith. We can resist his attacks, knowing that we are equipped with the armor of God and the strength of the Holy Spirit.

Practical Applications

To rely on God's power in our daily lives, we must engage in practices that deepen our relationship with Him. This includes prayer, worship, and studying Scripture. By cultivating a strong connection with God, we can draw strength and wisdom to navigate life's challenges.

The Power of Prayer

Prayer is a powerful tool that connects us with God's strength. When we pray, we acknowledge our dependence on Him and invite His intervention in our lives. When our spirit is connected to God we have the power to do all things, and defeat all enemies.

Pray Boldly: Approach God with confidence, knowing that He hears your prayers and desires to respond.

Pray with Purpose: Be specific in your prayers, asking God for guidance, strength, and clarity in your situations.

Reflection Questions

How can you deepen your understanding of God's sovereignty in your life?

In what ways have you experienced God's power in your own journey?

How can you incorporate prayer more intentionally into your daily routine?

Chapter 9

Top Gun Training for Christians

Essential Qualities for Spiritual Warfare

To be effective in spiritual warfare, Christians must develop key qualities such as vigilance, knowledge, and resilience. These attributes are not developed overnight; they require intentional effort and commitment.

Vigilance involves being aware of the enemy's tactics and recognizing when we are under attack. Knowledge comes from studying Scripture and understanding God's truth, while resilience is built through facing challenges and learning to trust God in difficult times.

2 Timothy 2:15: "Do your best to present yourself to God as one approved, a worker who does not need to be ashamed and who correctly handles the word of truth."

Spiritual Disciplines

Engaging in spiritual disciplines is vital for preparation. Regular prayer, fasting, and Bible study are essential practices that strengthen our faith and equip us for battle.

Consider how a pilot prepares for a mission: they study flight manuals, practice maneuvers, and engage in simulations. Similarly, Christians must immerse themselves in God's Word and seek His guidance through God's truths and prayer to be ready for the spiritual battles ahead.

Jeremiah 29:11-13 (New King James Version): "For I know the thoughts that I think toward you, says the Lord, thoughts of peace and not of evil, to give you a future and a hope. Then you will call upon Me and go and pray to Me, and I will listen to you. And you will seek Me and find Me, when you search for Me with all your heart."

Real-Life Examples

Throughout Scripture, we see examples of individuals who faced spiritual battles with courage and faith. For instance, Esther risked her life to save her people, demonstrating resilience and trust in God. These stories serve as powerful reminders that we can draw strength from our faith in God as we confront our own challenges.

Developing a Battle Plan

Just as military leaders develop battle plans, Christians should create a spiritual battle plan. This plan can include:

Identifying Weaknesses:

Recognize areas in your life where you are vulnerable to temptation or doubt.

Setting Goals: Establish spiritual goals that align with your faith journey, such as reading through the Bible or increasing your prayer life.

Accountability Partners: Seek out friends or mentors who can support you and hold you accountable in your spiritual growth.

Psalm 144: "Praise be to the Lord my Rock, who trains my hands for war, my fingers for battle."

Reflection Questions

What qualities do you need to develop to be more effective in spiritual warfare?

How can you incorporate spiritual disciplines into your daily life?

Who can you turn to for support and accountability in your faith journey?

Chapter 10

Spiritual Commitment

Being a "Top Gun" for God requires a deep commitment to spiritual growth. This commitment involves setting aside distractions and prioritizing our relationship with God. It may require sacrifices, but the rewards are immeasurable.

1 Corinthians 9:25: "Everyone who competes in the games goes into strict training."

Reflect on your spiritual journey and consider areas where you can deepen your commitment. Are there habits or distractions that hinder your growth? Identifying these obstacles is the first step toward overcoming them.

1 Timothy 4:7: "Have nothing to do with godless myths and old wives' tales; rather, train yourself to be godly."

Building a Supportive Community

Community plays a vital role in spiritual commitment. Surrounding ourselves with fellow believers provides encouragement and accountability. When we share our struggles and victories, we strengthen one another's faith.

Consider joining a small group or Bible study where you can engage in meaningful discussions and support each other's growth. These relationships can provide a sense of belonging and purpose as you navigate your faith journey.

Living with Purpose

As you pursue spiritual commitment, seek to identify your God-given purpose. Each believer has a unique calling, and living in alignment with that purpose brings fulfillment and joy.

Take time to pray and reflect on how God is calling you to serve others and glorify Him. Whether it's through acts of kindness, sharing the Gospel, or using your talents in ministry, embracing your purpose will enhance your spiritual journey.

2 Timothy 3:16: "All Scripture is God-breathed and is useful for teaching, rebuking, correcting and training in righteousness,"

Practical Steps for Commitment

Daily Reflection: Set aside time each day to reflect on your spiritual journey and seek God's guidance.

Service Opportunities: Look for ways to serve in your community, whether through volunteering or helping those in need.

Regular Check-Ins: Schedule regular check-ins with a mentor or accountability partner to discuss your spiritual growth.

Reflection Questions

What specific commitments do you need to make to grow spiritually?

How can you actively seek out community support in your faith journey?

In what ways can you live out your God-given purpose daily?

Chapter 11

Top Gun Daily Training

Commitment to Spiritual Training

To be a "Top Gun" for God, daily training is essential. Just as elite pilots engage in rigorous practice to hone their skills, Christians must commit to spiritual disciplines that deepen their faith and prepare them for spiritual battles. This chapter outlines key areas for daily training that will help believers grow in their relationship with God.

Study God's Word

The Bible is the foundational text for understanding God's will and principles for living a life that honors Him. Regular engagement with Scripture is vital for spiritual growth. It is through the Word that believers learn about God's character, His promises, and the teachings of Jesus.

1 Timothy 4:8: "For physical training is of some value, but godliness has value for all things, holding promise for both the present life and the life to come."

Consider setting aside dedicated time each day for Bible study. This could be in the morning to start your day with God or in the evening to reflect on His Word. Journaling your insights can enhance your understanding and help you apply biblical principles to your life.

Hebrews 5:14: "But solid food is for the mature, who by constant use have trained themselves to distinguish good from evil."

Practical Application:

Choose a specific book of the Bible to study in depth. For example, if you choose the Book of James, focus on its teachings about faith and works. Take notes on each chapter, highlighting key verses that resonate with you.

Prayer

Prayer is the lifeline for believers, providing a direct line of communication with God. It is in prayer that we seek guidance, express gratitude, and request strength for the challenges we face. Establishing a consistent prayer routine can transform your spiritual life.

Incorporate various forms of prayer, including adoration, confession, thanksgiving, and supplication (ACTS). This holistic approach allows for a richer prayer experience. Additionally, consider using prayer prompts or guided prayers to help you stay focused and intentional.

Practical Application:

Create a prayer journal where you record your prayers, answers, and reflections. This practice not only helps you track your spiritual journey but also encourages gratitude as you see how God responds.

Obedience to God's Commands

A Top Gun pilot must adhere to strict protocols to ensure mission success. Similarly, Christians are called to obey God's commandments. This obedience reflects our love for God and our commitment to His ways.

Take time to reflect on areas in your life where you may struggle with obedience. Are there commands you find difficult to follow? Seek God's help through prayer and accountability with fellow believers to strengthen your resolve.

Practical Application:

Identify one commandment or biblical principle to focus on each week. Create a plan for how you will implement this principle in your daily life.

Hebrews 12:11: "No discipline seems pleasant at the time, but painful. Later on, however, it produces a harvest of righteousness and peace for those who have been trained by it."

Developing Godly Character

Godly character is essential for spiritual growth. Key attributes such as integrity, perseverance, humility, and compassion should be cultivated through daily practice.

For instance, integrity involves being honest and consistent in your actions, even when no one is watching. Look for opportunities to demonstrate integrity in your workplace, relationships, and community.

Practical Application:

Set a goal to practice one specific attribute of godly character each week. For example, focus on humility by serving others in your community or workplace.

Surrounding Yourself with Fellow Believers

Just as pilots depend on their squadron for support, Christians need a community of fellow believers to walk alongside them. Engaging in fellowship through church, Bible studies, or small groups provides encouragement, accountability, and opportunities for growth.

Consider joining a small group where you can share your struggles and victories with others. These relationships can provide the support needed to navigate spiritual challenges and encourage one another in faith.

Practical Application:

Attend a church event or join a small group where you can build relationships with fellow believers. Make it a goal to connect with at least one new person each week.

Reflection Questions

What does being a "Top Gun" for God mean to you personally?

In what ways have you experienced spiritual warfare in your own life?

How can you prepare yourself for the battles you face in your faith journey?

Chapter 12

Confronting Discouragement and Doubt

Understanding the Temptation

Discouragement and doubt are common challenges that Christians face at various points in their spiritual journeys. These feelings can arise from personal struggles, unanswered prayers, or the weight of life's challenges.

For example, consider John, a devoted Christian who has been fervently praying for a breakthrough in his finances. Just when he feels hopeful, he faces an unexpected financial crisis. In this vulnerable moment, Satan whispers lies that seek to shake his faith, such as:

"God doesn't care about you."

"Your prayers are worthless."

"You're a failure; nothing will ever change."

"If God truly loved you, He would have helped you by now."

These thoughts can lead John to feel isolated, anxious, and tempted to abandon his faith.

Recognizing the Attack

The first step in overcoming discouragement is recognizing it as a tactic of the enemy. Understanding that these feelings are not from God can empower believers to combat them. Scripture reminds us that God is a source of hope and encouragement, not despair.

Hebrews 5:14: "But solid food is for the mature, who by constant use have trained themselves to distinguish good from evil."

Practical Application:

Keep a journal of your feelings and thoughts during times of doubt. Writing them down can help you identify patterns and recognize when you are under spiritual attack.

Counter-Tactics for Overcoming Doubt

To effectively counter the lies of the enemy, John can employ several spiritual strategies:

Stand on God's Promises (Belt of Truth): John counters the enemy's lies by grounding himself in the truth of God's Word. He recalls powerful scriptures that affirm God's faithfulness and provision.

Philippians 4:19: "And my God will supply every need of yours according to his riches in glory in Christ Jesus."

Jeremiah 29:11: "For I know the plans I have for you," declares the Lord, "plans to prosper you and not to harm you, plans to give you hope and a future."

By declaring these promises aloud and meditating on them, John renews his mind and shifts his focus back to God's power and goodness.

Pray with Faith (Shield of Faith): Despite the temptation to give in to despair, John chooses to pray fervently. By lifting his financial concerns to God, he activates his shield of faith, blocking the fiery darts of doubt.

James 1:5-6: "If any of you lacks wisdom, let him ask of God, who gives generously to all without reproach, and it will be given to him."

Praise and Thank God (Helmet of Salvation): Instead of dwelling on his crisis, John chooses to focus on gratitude. He remembers that his salvation is secure, and no temporary hardship can take that away.

1 Thessalonians 5:18: "Give thanks in all circumstances; for this is the will of God in Christ Jesus for you."

By praising God for His past faithfulness, John protects his mind with the helmet of salvation, allowing him to rise above immediate challenges and see things from an eternal perspective.

Seek Encouragement from Fellow Believers (Community Support): Recognizing that isolation can intensify discouragement, John reaches out to his Bible study group for prayer and support. Fellow believers lift him up, reminding him that he is not alone in this battle.

Hebrews 10:25: "Not neglecting to meet together, as is the habit of some, but encouraging one another, and all the more as you see the Day drawing near."

Engage in Acts of Service (Counteracting Self-Focus): Sometimes, focusing on others can help alleviate feelings of discouragement. John volunteers at a local charity, helping those in need. This act of service shifts his perspective and reminds him of God's blessings.

Reflection Questions

How do you typically respond to feelings of discouragement?

What promises from God can you cling to during difficult times?

In what ways can you seek support from your community when facing doubt?

Chapter 13

Battling Lust and Sexual Sin

Understanding the Temptation

In this chapter, we confront the powerful temptation of lust and sexual sin. Consider Sarah, a strong believer who reconnects with an old friend who shows romantic interest. The attraction is strong, and while she knows God's standard for purity, Satan begins to whisper lies:

"It's okay; you're both consenting adults."

"God will forgive you, just this once."

"You deserve to feel good, and no one will ever know."

These thoughts can lead Sarah to rationalize her behavior, tempting her to compromise her values.

Recognizing the Attack

Sarah recognizes that these temptations are spiritual attacks meant to lead her away from God's standards.

Understanding this is crucial for her to combat the lies effectively.

Practical Application:

Consider journaling about your feelings and thoughts when faced with temptation. This practice can help you identify triggers and patterns in your behavior.

Counter-Tactics for Overcoming Temptation

To resist the temptation of lust, Sarah employs several strategies:

Flee from the Situation (Sword of the Spirit and Shield of Faith): Sarah remembers **1 Corinthians 6:18**, which instructs believers to "flee from sexual immorality." Instead of engaging with the temptation, she chooses to remove herself from the situation.

Fill Her Mind with Scripture (Helmet of Salvation and Belt of Truth): Sarah immerses herself in God's Word, meditating on verses that emphasize purity and holiness, such as:

1 Thessalonians 4:3-4: "For this is the will of God, your sanctification: that you abstain from sexual immorality; that each one of you know how to control his own body in holiness and honor."

Rely on the Holy Spirit's Strength (Prayer and Dependence): Sarah prays for the strength to resist temptation, acknowledging her dependence on the Holy Spirit for guidance and support.

Accountability (Community and Transparency):

Sarah reaches out to a trusted accountability partner, sharing her struggle. This openness allows her to receive prayer and encouragement, reinforcing her commitment to purity.

Guarding Her Heart (Preventative Measures):

After successfully navigating the temptation, Sarah takes proactive steps to avoid similar situations in the future. She sets boundaries in her relationships and increases her time spent in prayer and Scripture.

Reflection Questions

What specific strategies can you implement to guard against lust and sexual sin?

How can accountability relationships strengthen your resolve in maintaining purity?

In what ways can you fill your mind with Scripture to combat temptation?

Chapter 14

Resisting Pride and Self-Sufficiency

Understanding the Temptation

In this chapter, we explore the subtle yet dangerous temptation of pride and self-sufficiency. Meet David, a successful businessman who begins to feel a sense of self-importance due to his achievements. As accolades and praise pour in, David starts to rely more on his abilities and less on God.

Satan exploits this vulnerability, planting thoughts in David's mind:

"Look at all you've accomplished! You're a self-made success."

"You don't need to depend on God as much anymore."

"You're better than others who haven't achieved what you have."

Recognizing these thoughts as spiritual attacks is essential for David as he navigates his success.

Counter-Tactics for Overcoming Pride

To combat pride, David employs several strategies:

Humble Himself Before God (Belt of Truth and Shield of Faith): David recalls **James 4:6**, which states that God opposes the proud but gives grace to the humble. He chooses to acknowledge that all his success comes from God's grace, not his own merit.

Reflect on God's Greatness (Worship and Praise): To combat feelings of self-importance, David spends time in worship, focusing on God's majesty and sovereignty. He remembers **Psalm 24:1**, which reminds him that everything belongs to the Lord.

Remember His Dependence on God (Prayer and Surrender): David takes time to pray and surrender his future plans to God. He seeks guidance and acknowledges that without God, he can accomplish nothing of eternal value.

Generosity and Serving Others (Guarding Against Pride): To guard against pride, David actively seeks opportunities to serve others. He understands that true greatness comes from humility and selflessness.

Accountability and Wise Counsel (Iron Sharpens Iron): David reaches out to a trusted mentor to discuss his struggles with pride. This accountability helps him stay grounded and focused on what truly matters.

Reflection Questions

In what areas of your life do you struggle with pride or self-sufficiency?

How can you actively practice humility in your daily interactions?

Who can you turn to for guidance and accountability in your faith journey?

Chapter 15

Overcoming Anger and Unforgiveness

Understanding the Temptation

In this chapter, we confront the temptation of anger and unforgiveness. Sarah finds herself deeply hurt after a close friend betrays her trust by spreading a rumor. As she grapples with her emotions, Satan attempts to exploit her pain, whispering lies that encourage her to hold onto anger:

"You have every right to be angry."

"They don't deserve your forgiveness."

"Stay mad and let them feel your wrath."

Recognizing these thoughts as spiritual attacks is crucial for Sarah as she navigates her feelings.

Counter-Tactics for Forgiveness

To combat anger and unforgiveness, Sarah employs several strategies:

Choosing to Forgive (Sword of the Spirit and Shield of Faith): Sarah understands that forgiving others is not optional for Christians. She recalls **Matthew 6:14-15**, which emphasizes the importance of forgiving others to receive God's forgiveness. By choosing to forgive, she actively resists the enemy's lies.

Praying for Her Friend (Praying with a Pure Heart): Instead of dwelling on her anger, Sarah begins to pray for her friend. This act of prayer softens her heart and opens her to the healing power of the Holy Spirit.

Releasing the Hurt to God (Casting Her Burdens on the Lord): Acknowledging her pain, Sarah pours out her feelings to God in prayer. She releases the burden of her hurt, trusting that God will heal her heart.

Guarding Her Heart (Refusing to Dwell on the Offense): Sarah takes control of her thoughts by refusing to dwell on the offense. She fills her mind with thoughts of God's goodness and grace.

Seeking Reconciliation (Pursuing Peace): Sarah doesn't just forgive her friend privately; she also seeks reconciliation. She remembers **Romans 12:18**, which encourages believers to live at peace with everyone. By reaching out for an honest conversation, she removes the enemy's foothold in their relationship.

Reflection Questions

How can you actively choose to forgive those who have wronged you?

In what ways can prayer help you overcome feelings of anger?

What steps can you take to pursue reconciliation in broken relationships?

Chapter 16

Battling Fear and Anxiety

Understanding the Temptation

This chapter focuses on the temptation of fear and anxiety, illustrating the struggles faced by John, a faithful Christian who experiences sudden job loss. As financial pressures mount, Satan attempts to instill fear and doubt in John's mind:

"How will you survive without income?"

"God has abandoned you."

"What if things never get better?"

Recognizing these thoughts as spiritual attacks is essential for John as he navigates this difficult season.

Counter-Tactics for Overcoming Fear

To combat fear and anxiety, John employs several strategies:

Trusting in God's Sovereignty (Shield of Faith and Helmet of Salvation): John reminds himself of God's control over every situation. He meditates on **Romans 8:28**, which reassures him that God works all things for good.

Replacing Lies with God's Truth (Sword of the Spirit): John counters the enemy's lies by filling his mind with Scripture. He recalls **Philippians 4:19**, which promises that God will supply all his needs.

Casting His Anxiety on God (Prayer and Supplication): John turns to prayer, pouring out his fears and worries to God. He follows **1 Peter 5:7**, which encourages believers to cast their anxieties on the Lord.

Practicing Gratitude (Rejoicing in the Lord): Despite his circumstances, John chooses to practice gratitude. He thanks God for the blessings he still has, shifting his focus from fear to thankfulness.

Staying in Community (Accountability and Encouragement): John knows that Satan often uses isolation to intensify fear and anxiety. He reaches out to his church community for support, sharing his struggles and asking for prayer. His friends in Christ encourage him with Scripture, pray over him, and remind him of God's faithfulness.

Reflection Questions

How do you typically respond to fear and anxiety in your life?

What specific Scriptures can you memorize to combat fear?

How can community support play a role in overcoming anxiety?

Chapter 17

Resisting the Temptation to Lie or Deceive

Understanding the Temptation

In this chapter, the author addresses the temptation to lie and deceive, introducing Susan, a Christian working in a competitive corporate environment. After making a mistake on an important project, Susan feels pressured to cover up her error rather than admit it.

Satan whispers deceptive thoughts, attempting to lure her into dishonesty:

"It's just a small lie—no one will ever know."

"If you admit your mistake, you'll get fired."

"Everyone else bends the truth to protect themselves."

Recognizing these thoughts as spiritual attacks is crucial for Susan as she navigates her integrity.

Counter-Tactics for Upholding Integrity

To combat the temptation to lie, Susan employs several strategies:

Speaking Truth (Belt of Truth and Sword of the Spirit): Susan understands the importance of honesty. She recalls **Ephesians 4:25**, which instructs believers to speak truthfully. By choosing to tell the truth, she resists the enemy's lies.

Trusting God for the Outcome (Shield of Faith): Despite her fears, Susan decides to trust God with the consequences of her honesty. She remembers **Proverbs 3:5-6**, which encourages believers to lean on God's understanding.

Praying for Strength (Helmet of Salvation): Knowing that honesty might bring immediate difficulty, Susan prays for strength and wisdom.

Philippians 4:6-7 comes to mind, reminding her that God's peace will guard her heart.

Seeking Accountability (Community and Transparency): Susan reaches out to a trusted Christian friend to share her struggle. This accountability helps her stay grounded and focused on her values.

Choosing Integrity Over Convenience: In every situation, Susan commits to choosing integrity over convenience. She understands that short-term gains from dishonesty can lead to long-term consequences.

Reflection Questions

How can you cultivate a habit of honesty in your daily life?

What fears do you have about being truthful in challenging situations?

Who can you turn to for support in maintaining your integrity?

Chapter 18

Satan's Cycle of Confusion,Lies, Hate, and Violence

Understanding the Dangerous Path from Deception to Destruction

In the realm of human interaction, the power of communication cannot be overstated. Words can heal, inspire, and unite, yet they can also deceive, manipulate, and destroy. Among the most pernicious tactics employed in this darker spectrum is the creation of confusion. By deliberately sowing seeds of doubt and ambiguity, individuals or groups can manipulate perceptions, making it easier to propagate falsehoods. This weaponization of confusion can set off a chain reaction that ultimately leads to hate and violence.

Creating Confusion

Confusion is a state of mind where clarity is absent and understanding is clouded. It can be deliberately induced through misinformation, contradictory statements, and ambiguous language. When people are confused, they become uncertain and seek guidance or explanations that provide a semblance of order. This vulnerability makes them susceptible to manipulation.

One of the key techniques in creating confusion is the spread of misinformation—false or misleading information presented as fact. By bombarding individuals with conflicting reports, half-truths, and outright lies, manipulators can erode trust in credible sources. This tactic is particularly effective in the digital age, where the rapid dissemination of information through social media can overwhelm individuals, making it difficult to discern truth from falsehood.

The Weaponization of Confusion

Once confusion has taken root, it becomes a potent weapon for those seeking to deceive. Amidst the fog of uncertainty, a lie can be strategically introduced as a beacon of clarity. The lie offers a simple, often emotionally charged explanation that cuts through the confusion. This clarity, albeit false, is appealing to those desperate for answers.

The lie is further reinforced through repetition and selective evidence. Manipulators may cherry-pick information, amplify anecdotes, and create echo chambers where the lie is continuously affirmed. Over time, repeated exposure to the lie strengthens its perceived validity, leading people to accept it as truth.

The Birth of Hate

Lies often play on existing biases and fears, magnifying them to create a sense of threat or injustice. This emotional manipulation can give rise to hate. For instance, a lie that blames a particular group for societal or personal hardships can incite feelings of anger and resentment. The simplicity of the lie and its emotional appeal makes it a powerful tool for fostering division.

Hate is a potent emotion that thrives on the dehumanization of its target. The lie serves to strip away the complexity and humanity of the targeted group, reducing them to a monolithic enemy responsible for all wrongs. This dehumanization is crucial, as it lowers the moral and psychological barriers that typically prevent individuals from endorsing or committing acts of aggression.

The Escalation to Violence

As hate takes hold, it can manifest in violent actions. The narrative constructed by the lie justifies and even glorifies these actions as necessary and righteous. Violence becomes a means of addressing the perceived threat or injustice, and those who perpetrate it see themselves as defenders of a greater good.

History is replete with examples of this dangerous progression. From ethnic cleansing to terrorism, the trajectory often starts with confusion and misinformation, escalates to hate fueled by lies, and culminates in violence. The consequences are devastating, not only for the immediate victims but also for the broader society, as the cycle of violence and retribution can be perpetuated indefinitely.

Breaking the Cycle

To prevent the cycle of confusion, lies, hate, and violence, it is imperative to promote media literacy and critical thinking. Educating individuals on how to verify information, recognize biases, and analyze sources can fortify them against manipulation. Additionally, fostering open and respectful dialogue can help bridge divides and reduce the allure of simplistic, divisive narratives.

Trust in credible institutions and the promotion of transparency are also key. When people have faith in the integrity of their information sources, they are less likely to fall prey to confusion and deception. Finally, addressing the root causes of societal grievances—such as inequality, injustice, and disenfranchisement—can reduce the fertile ground on which lies and hate flourish.

In conclusion, the deliberate creation of confusion is a dangerous tactic that can lead individuals down a path of deception, hate, and violence. By understanding this progression and taking proactive steps to foster clarity, critical thinking, and empathy, we can break the cycle and build a more informed, compassionate, and resilient society.

Contrasting God's Teachings with Satan's Cycle of Confusion, Lies, Hate and Violence

The Path to Healing and Peace

The Cycle of Confusion, Lies, Hate, and Violence

Lies often play on existing biases and fears, magnifying them to create a sense of threat or injustice. This emotional manipulation can give rise to hate. For instance, a lie that blames a particular group for societal or personal hardships can incite feelings of anger and resentment. The simplicity of the lie and its emotional appeal make it a powerful tool for fostering division.

Hate is a potent emotion that thrives on the dehumanization of its target. The lie serves to strip away the complexity and humanity of the targeted group, reducing them to a monolithic enemy responsible for all wrongs. This dehumanization is crucial, as it lowers the moral and psychological barriers that typically prevent individuals from endorsing or committing acts of aggression.

As hate takes hold, it can manifest in violent actions. The narrative constructed by the lie justifies and even glorifies these actions as necessary and righteous. Violence becomes a means of addressing the perceived threat or injustice, and those who perpetrate it see themselves as defenders of the greater good. History is replete with examples of this dangerous progression. From ethnic cleansing to terrorism, the trajectory often starts with confusion and misinformation, escalates to hate fueled by lies, and culminates in violence. The consequences are devastating, not only for the immediate victims but also for the broader society, as the cycle of violence and retribution can be perpetuated indefinitely.

To prevent the cycle of confusion, lies, hate, and violence, it is imperative to promote media literacy and critical thinking. Educating individuals on how to verify information, recognize biases, and analyze sources can fortify them against manipulation. Additionally, fostering open and respectful dialogue can help bridge divides and reduce the allure of simplistic, divisive narratives. Trust in credible institutions and the promotion of transparency are also key. When people have faith in the integrity of their information sources, they are less likely to fall prey to confusion and deception. Finally, addressing the root causes of societal grievances—such as inequality, injustice, and disenfranchisement—can reduce the fertile ground on which lies and hate flourish.

The Teachings of God: Path to Healing

The teachings of God, as expressed through various religious traditions, provide a stark contrast to the destructive cycle of confusion, lies, hate, and violence. These teachings emphasize truth, love, compassion, and forgiveness, offering a path to healing for the mind, heart, and soul.

Embracing Truth

At the core of God's teachings is the pursuit of truth. In many religious texts, truth is equated with divine wisdom and enlightenment. For example, in Christianity, Jesus Christ proclaimed, "I am the way, the truth, and the life" **(John 14:6).** The pursuit of truth involves honest self-reflection, integrity in communication, and a commitment to seeking knowledge. By embracing truth, individuals can dispel confusion and deception, creating a foundation for understanding and harmony.

Choosing Love Over Hate

God's teachings consistently advocate for love as the highest virtue. Love is seen as a transformative force that can heal wounds, bridge divides, and foster unity. In the Bible, Jesus emphasizes the importance of love, stating, "Love your neighbor as yourself" **(Mark 12:31).** This principle encourages individuals to see the humanity in others, even those who may be different or hold opposing views. By choosing love over hate, people can overcome biases and prejudices, cultivating a spirit of inclusivity and acceptance.

Practicing Compassion and Forgiveness

Compassion and forgiveness are essential teachings in many religious traditions. Compassion involves recognizing the suffering of others and taking action to alleviate it. In Buddhism, the concept of "karuna" (compassion) is central to the path of enlightenment. Forgiveness, on the other hand, involves letting go of resentment and anger toward those who have wronged us. In Islam, forgiveness is highly valued, with the Quran stating, "But if you pardon and overlook and forgive – then indeed, Allah is Forgiving and Merciful" **(Quran 64:14).** By practicing compassion and forgiveness, individuals can break the cycle of retribution and violence, fostering healing and reconciliation.

Promoting Peace and Non-Violence

God's teachings often emphasize the importance of peace and non-violence. In Hinduism, the principle of "ahimsa" (non-violence) is a foundational ethic that promoting respect for all living beings. Similarly, in Christianity, Jesus teaches, "Blessed are the peacemakers, for they will be called children of God" **(Matthew 5:9).** The promotion of peace involves addressing conflicts through dialogue, understanding, and cooperation rather than resorting to aggression and hostility. By prioritizing peace, individuals can create environments where healing and growth are possible.

Conclusion

The teachings of God offer a powerful antidote to the cycle of confusion, lies, hate, and violence. By embracing truth, choosing love over hate, practicing compassion and forgiveness, and promoting peace and non-violence, individuals can find healing for their minds, hearts, and souls. These divine principles provide a path to a more informed, compassionate, and resilient society, where understanding and empathy prevail over division and hostility.

Top Guns for God:

Using Divine Wisdom to Defeat Confusion and Lies An Exploration of Spiritual Warfare

Embracing Truth

At the forefront of their mission, Top Guns for God strive to uphold the principle of truth. They recognize that truth is synonymous with divine wisdom and enlightenment. In Christianity, Jesus Christ declared, "I am the way, the truth, and the life" **(John 14:6).** By embracing truth, they engage in honest self-reflection, communicate with integrity, and commit to seeking knowledge. This dedication to truth dispels the darkness of confusion and deception, laying a solid foundation for understanding and harmony.

Choosing Love Over Hate

In the battle against Satan's lies, Top Guns for God prioritize love as the highest virtue. They understand that love is a transformative force capable of healing wounds, bridging divides, and fostering unity. Jesus emphasized the importance of love, stating, "Love your neighbor as yourself" **(Mark 12:31).** By choosing love over hate, they encourage people to see the humanity in others, even those who may differ in beliefs or perspectives.

This principle helps overcome biases and prejudices, nurturing a spirit of inclusivity and acceptance.

Practicing Compassion and Forgiveness

Compassion and forgiveness are essential weapons in the arsenal of Top Guns for God. Compassion involves recognizing the suffering of others and taking steps to alleviate it, while forgiveness entails letting go of resentment and anger. In Buddhism, the concept of "karuna" (compassion) is central to the path of enlightenment. Similarly, in Islam, forgiveness is highly valued, as highlighted in the Quran, "But if you pardon and overlook and forgive – then indeed, Allah is Forgiving and Merciful" **(Quran 64:14)**. By practicing compassion and forgiveness, they break the cycle of retribution and violence, fostering healing and reconciliation.

Promoting Peace and Non-Violence

Top Guns for God emphasizes the importance of peace and non-violence, understanding that these principles are crucial in defeating Satan's traps. In Hinduism, the principle of "ahimsa" (non-violence) promotes respect for all living beings. Christianity echoes this sentiment with Jesus' teaching, "Blessed are the peacemakers, for they will be called children of God" **(Matthew 5:9).** They address conflicts through dialogue, understanding, and cooperation, rather than aggression. By prioritizing peace, they create environments where healing and growth are possible.

Conclusion

Top Guns for God use their Godly wisdom to defeat the confusion and lies that Satan employs to trap innocent people. By embracing divine principles—truth, love, compassion, forgiveness, peace, and non-violence—they pave the way for a more informed, compassionate, and resilient society. In their spiritual warfare, they offer a powerful antidote to the cycle of deception and hostility, fostering understanding and empathy in the face of division.

Essential Biblical Scriptures for Top Guns for God

Teaching Others to Overcome Satan's Confusion, Lies, Hate, and Violence

Introduction

In the spiritual warfare against Satan's deception and malevolence, it is vital for a Top Gun for God to be equipped with powerful biblical scriptures that offer guidance, wisdom, and strength. These scriptures help individuals to resist confusion, lies, hate, and violence, fostering a spirit of truth, love, compassion, and peace.

Embracing Truth

Truth is a cornerstone of divine wisdom, and it is essential for dispelling confusion and deception. The following scriptures underline the importance of truth:

- **John 14:6:** "I am the way, the truth, and the life."

- **John 8:32:** "Then you will know the truth, and the truth will set you free."

- **Proverbs 12:19:** "Truthful lips endure forever, but a lying tongue lasts only a moment."

Choosing Love Over Hate

Love is the highest virtue in God's teachings, a force that can heal and unite. These scriptures emphasize the transformative power of love:

- **Mark 12:31:** "Love your neighbor as yourself."

- **1 Corinthians 13:4-7:** "Love is patient, love is kind. It does not envy, it does not boast, it is not proud. It does not dishonor others, it is not self-seeking, it is not easily angered, it keeps no record of wrongs. Love does not delight in evil but rejoices with the truth. It always protects, always trusts, always hopes, always perseveres."

- **1 John 4:8:** "Whoever does not love does not know God, because God is love."

Practicing Compassion and Forgiveness

Compassion and forgiveness are vital for breaking the cycle of retribution and fostering healing. The following scriptures highlight their importance:

- **Luke 6:36:** "Be merciful, just as your Father is merciful."

- **Ephesians 4:32:** "Be kind and compassionate to one another, forgiving each other, just as in Christ God forgave you."

- **Matthew 6:14-15:** "For if you forgive other people when they sin against you, your heavenly Father will also forgive you. But if you do not forgive others their sins, your Father will not forgive your sins."

Promoting Peace and Non-Violence

Peace and non-violence are essential for resolving conflicts and promoting harmony. These scriptures advocate for peace:

- **Matthew 5:9:** "Blessed are the peacemakers, for they will be called children of God."

- **Romans 12:18:** "If it is possible, as far as it depends on you, live at peace with everyone."

- **Hebrews 12:14:** "Make every effort to live in peace with everyone and to be holy; without holiness no one will see the Lord."

Conclusion

Equipped with these powerful biblical scriptures, Top Guns for God can effectively teach others how to resist Satan's confusion, lies, hate, and violence. Embracing truth, choosing love, practicing compassion and forgiveness, and promoting peace provide a path to a more enlightened, harmonious, and resilient society, where divine principles prevail over division and hostility.

Chapter 19

The Power of God Stories

So, what is a God story, or how do our God Stories relate to being a Top Gun for God and helping others?

Our personal God stories—the experiences of how God has worked in our lives—play a powerful role in helping others grow closer to Him. These stories, often referred to as testimonies, are unique and deeply personal accounts of faith, transformation, and God's presence in everyday life. When we share these stories, we can inspire, encourage, and lead others toward a deeper relationship with God and help them to become God-fearing, Satan beating, Top Guns for God. Here's how:

1. Testimonies Make God Real and Relatable

Many people can find it difficult to connect with abstract theological concepts or distant ideas about God. However, when they hear real-life examples of how God has intervened in someone's life, it makes God more tangible and relatable.

Personal stories humanize faith. They allow others to see that God is not just an idea but a living, active presence who works in the lives of real people. For example, if you share how God provided for you in a difficult time or how He healed a relationship, it can demonstrate His faithfulness and care in ways that theology or doctrine alone might not communicate.

2. They Show God's Transformative Power

God's stories highlight how God transforms lives. Whether it's a dramatic story of salvation, deliverance from addiction, healing from pain, or gradual spiritual growth, these testimonies reveal God's power to change hearts and circumstances.

Transformation encourages others. When someone sees that God has helped you overcome a personal struggle, it offers them hope that God can do the same for them. It shows that God is active, loving, and powerful enough to intervene in their own challenges.

3. They Offer Hope in Difficult Times

Personal stories of overcoming trials through God's grace can offer hope to people going through their own struggles. When people hear how God was faithful during someone else's hardship, it reassures them that He will not abandon them in their time of need.

Your testimony can offer comfort and peace, showing others that even in the darkest moments, God is present. This can inspire them to trust God more deeply and persevere through difficult seasons in life.

4. They Break Down Barriers

Many people may have preconceived notions about faith or feel distant from God due to doubts, skepticism, or past hurts. Personal stories can break down those barriers because they aren't about debating doctrine or forcing beliefs but simply sharing what God has done in your life.

Testimonies are powerful because they come from a place of personal experience. People may argue against theological ideas, but it's much harder to dismiss a personal story. When you share authentically, it can soften hearts and open doors to deeper conversations about faith.

5. They Encourage Faith and Trust in God

Hearing about how God worked in someone's life encourages others to trust God in their own circumstances. It reinforces the idea that God is trustworthy, faithful, and involved in the details of our lives.

For example, if you share how God answered a specific prayer or led you through a confusing season, it encourages others to bring their needs to God and trust in His timing and wisdom. Your story becomes a testament to God's faithfulness, encouraging them to lean into their own relationship with Him.

6. They Help People See Their Own God Stories

When we share our experiences of God at work, it helps others recognize God's activity in their own lives. Sometimes, people may not realize that

God is already working in their lives until they hear a testimony that resonates with their experience.

Hearing someone else's story can prompt reflection and help others see their blessings, answered prayers, or moments when God was guiding them, even if they hadn't recognized it at the time.

7. They Build Community and Shared Faith

Sharing our God stories builds a sense of community and connection. When we open up about how God has worked in our lives, we invite others to share their stories, too. This creates an atmosphere of mutual support and encouragement.

In a community of believers, these stories can strengthen the collective faith of the group. Hearing how God has moved in the lives of others can energize a church or fellowship, bringing people closer to each other and to God.

8. They Overcome Fear and Isolation

People often feel alone in their struggles, but when we share our God stories, especially ones that involve overcoming adversity, it helps others realize they're not alone. Whether it's a battle with addiction, a difficult relationship, or a season of doubt, knowing that someone else has walked a similar path—and emerged with a stronger faith—can be incredibly encouraging.

Vulnerability breaks isolation. By sharing the real challenges we've faced and how God brought us through them, we create a safe space for others to open up and trust God with their own fears, doubts, or pain.

9. They Reflect the Gospel Message

Every God story ultimately points back to the Gospel—God's love, grace, and redemption. Personal testimonies are often modern-day illustrations of the core truths of Christianity: forgiveness, transformation, and hope through Christ.

When we share our story of how God's love has impacted us, it becomes a living testimony of the Gospel. It reflects the truth of Jesus' work in our lives, showing others that the Gospel is not just an ancient story but a living reality that changes lives today.

10. They Inspire Action and Faithfulness

Hearing how God has called someone to take a leap of faith, serve others, or step into a new direction can inspire others to be obedient to God's calling in their own lives. Testimonies often challenge others to take action in their faith, whether it's serving, praying, or simply trusting God in a deeper way.

God stories spark courage. If you share how God guided you through a significant decision or called you to a mission, it might be the encouragement someone else needs to take a step of faith in their own life.

11. They Glorify God

Ultimately, sharing our stories of God's work in our lives brings glory to Him. When we publicly acknowledge how God has moved in our lives— whether through healing, provision, or spiritual growth—we point others toward His greatness.

Psalm 105:1 says, "Give praise to the Lord, proclaim his name; make known among the nations what he has done." Our testimonies are a way of fulfilling this call, lifting up God's name, and drawing others toward His goodness.

Conclusion:

Sharing our God stories is one of the most powerful ways we can help others grow closer to God. Our experiences of His love, faithfulness, and transformation speak to the heart in ways that abstract teachings often cannot. They offer hope, build faith, and help others see that God is real, active, and personal.

By being open and vulnerable about how God has worked in our lives, we not only glorify Him but also invite others into their own deeper relationship with God. Each story shared becomes a bridge to greater faith, stronger trust, and a more personal understanding of God's presence in our lives.

How do you describe the greatness of God? Just look into a mirror, and you can see an image of God, and that leads to a myriad of both physical and invisible things he created, including you and me, all of mankind, and all living creatures. He is invisible yet omnipresent. He is in all parts of our lives. Without Him, we do not have life. He is the air you breath, and he is the pathway to eternal life. He has the whole world in his mighty hands. There is not a living soul that does not have a God story.

You might need to hear a few good ones to acknowledge some of your own. I share a few of my God stories in my book, "My God Stories- What's Yours." God Stories help you see how just how amazingly your life has been protected by the Hands of God. They are simple tools to help others see God's Hands at work, just like the simple parables Jesus used in his teachings.

My prayer is that we will fill the world with armies of highly motivated, strong Top Guns for God and many of His great stories.

For Top Guns in combat flight formations, there is always a flight lead. Everyone follows his calls. We need to recognize that we have God as our lead, and we need to develop good flight discipline and follow His lead in our lives.

Keep in mind God conceived Mary through the spirit, so there in nothing impossible with our God.

Jeremiah 29:11 (New International Version): "For I know the plans I have for you," declares the Lord, "plans to prosper you and not to harm you, plans to give you hope and a future."

Listen with your invisible ears, and you will hear His spirit speak to you, saying, "I have big plans for you, Top Gun."

I pray your God Stories will all be BEAUTIFUL.

Reflection Questions

How have you personally experienced God's transformative power in your life?

What stories can you share to encourage others in their faith journeys?

In what ways can you actively seek opportunities to share your testimony with others?

Chapter 20

What is a Love Basket

Love baskets are your best weapon. When you give out Love, you give God. In the realm of gift-giving, a "love basket" often serves as a thoughtful token of affection, embodying not just the physical items it contains but also the emotions and intentions behind it. A love basket typically includes a variety of curated items, often tailored to the preferences of the recipient, that together create a comprehensive expression of care and appreciation.

As we consider the impact of such personalized gifts, it is important to recognize how they resonate emotionally with individuals. The act of giving a love basket can forge deeper connections, reinforcing relationships through meaningful gestures. The items within the basket, whether they are gourmet treats, self-care products, or sentimental keepsakes, collectively communicate a narrative of thoughtfulness an understanding.

Looking ahead to the future of gift-giving, the concept of the love baske may evolve alongside advancements in technology. As we embrace digita platforms and online shopping, the ability to customize and personaliz these baskets is becoming more accessible. Virtual reality and augmente reality technologies could allow individuals to create a visua representation of their love basket before purchase, offering a mor interactive experience. Furthermore, the integration of artificia intelligence may enable gift-givers to receive personalized suggestion based on the recipient's preferences, enhancing the selection process.

In summary, a love basket is more than just a collection of items; it is modern expression of love that reflects the impact of persona connections.

With the ongoing evolution of technology, the future of creating an sharing such gifts promises to be even more engaging and meaningful.

Love baskets are a reflection of God.

Daily Mission of Love

Remember your daily mission: it is to rise up each morning with gratitud in your heart, thanking God for the gift of a new day filled wit opportunities and potential. As you step into the world, allow yourself t be guided down the path that God has laid out for you, embracing th journey ahead with an open mind and a willing spirit.

Each day presents a chance for you to empty your "Love Basket," whicl symbolizes the love, kindness, and compassion of God that you can shar with others. If Love is present, God is present. If God is present, Satal cannot be there.

This act is not merely a personal mission; it has a broader impact on thos around you. When you choose to spread love and positivity, yor contribute to a ripple effect that can transform your community an beyond. You give God when you give love. The simple gestures o kindness you extend can create waves of change, inspiring others to joil in this collective effort to uplift one another.

As we navigate the complexities of our lives, it's essential to recognize how these small acts of kindness can shape the future. In a world increasingly driven by technology, where interactions can sometimes feel impersonal and disconnected, the significance of human connection becomes even more pronounced. By consciously choosing to engage with others in meaningful ways, we remind ourselves and those around us of the warmth and empathy that lies at the core of our existence.

The pervasive nature of technology can often create barriers, making it easy to overlook the importance of personal connection. However, by intentionally fostering relationships and showing genuine interest in the lives of others, we can counteract this trend. Each conversation, each smile, and each act of kindness can serve as a powerful reminder that we are all part of a larger tapestry of humanity.

So, as you shine His light into the world, remember that your mission is not just about personal fulfillment; it is about harnessing the power of love in a rapidly evolving landscape. The choices you make today, the kindness you extend, and the light you share can have profound implications for how we navigate our interconnected lives tomorrow. In a future where technology continues to shape our interactions, your contributions can help foster a brighter, more compassionate world, reminding us all of the importance of empathy and connection amidst the digital noise.

Embrace this mission wholeheartedly, knowing that every act of kindness has the potential to create a lasting impact, not just in your immediate surroundings but also in shaping a future where love and compassion thrive. Together, we can cultivate an environment where technology serves to enhance our relationships rather than diminish them, paving the way for a more interconnected and harmonious society for generations to come. Give Love and give God and make the world a better place.

Love is the greatest counterattack to Satan; he runs from the presence of Love, which is God.

Conclusion

I would like to conclude by urging readers to embrace their roles as "Top Guns for God," equipped to face spiritual challenges with courage and faith. By sharing their God stories and leaning on the strength of the community, believers can encourage one another and make a significant impact in the world.

My prayer is that we will fill the world with armies of highly motivated strong Top Guns for God and many of His great stories.

For Top Guns in combat flight formations, there is always a flight lead. Everyone follows his calls. We need to recognize that we have God as our lead, and we need to develop good flight discipline and follow His lead in our lives.

Keep in mind God conceived Mary through the spirit, so there in nothing impossible with our God.

Jeremiah 29:11 (New International Version): "For I know the plans have for you, declares the Lord, plans to prosper you and not to harm you, plans to give you hope and a future."

Top Guns, listen with your invisible ears, and you will hear His spirit speak to you, saying, "I have big plans for you, Top Gun." Are you ready?

I pray for your success in becoming a Top Gun for God and that your God Stories will all be BEAUTIFUL.

Ephesians 2:10 (NLT): "For we are God's masterpiece. He has created us anew in Christ Jesus, so we can do the good things He planned for us long ago."

Being a masterpiece of God requires us to truly see that we are not just a coincidence; we are a purpose-driven creation of God.

He created you for a **"Mission Impossible,"** one that no other person can do. Do you accept this mission?

If you do not accept this mission, then this message will be erased in your mind in 10 seconds. If you accept this mission, God will lead you to your contacts today for you to share his goodness and his love. Good luck on completing your mission, Top Gun.

Sending God's Love to you!

Shadow